More great, original do-it-yourself projects
in the same series:

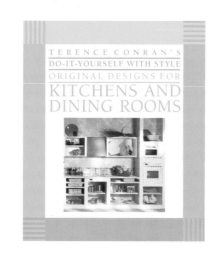

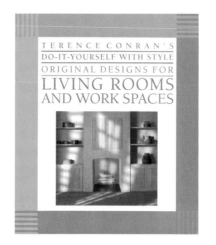

PROJECTS
The Kitchen System: Basic Units
Wall-mounted Shelf Unit
Plate Rack and Drip Tray
Knife Rack * Drying Rack
Serving and Display Unit with Mirrors
Divided Shelves
Hanging Bars
Suspended Shelves
Door Fronts

PROJECTS
Alcove Shelves and Cupboards
Radiator Cover
Wall of Display Shelving
Workbench
Tool Cupboard
Home Office
Workroom Ideas
Replacing Baseboards
Glass Shelves

TERENCE CONRAN'S
DO-IT-YOURSELF WITH STYLE
ORIGINAL DESIGNS FOR
BATHROOMS
AND BEDROOMS

CONSULTING EDITORS
JOHN McGOWAN AND ROGER DuBERN

PROJECT PHOTOGRAPHY BY HUGH JOHNSON

A FIRESIDE BOOK
PUBLISHED BY SIMON & SCHUSTER INC.
NEW YORK   LONDON   TORONTO   SYDNEY   TOKYO

F

FIRESIDE
Simon & Schuster Building
Rockefeller Center
1230 Avenue of the Americas
New York, New York 10020

First published in 1989 in Great Britain by
Conran Octopus Limited
37 Shelton Street, London WC2H 9HN

10 9 8 7 6 5 4 3 2 1

Library of Congress Cataloging in Publication Data

Conran, Terence.
    [Do-it-yourself with style]
    Terence Conran's do-it-yourself with style : original designs for
bathrooms and bedrooms / photography by Hugh Johnson.
        p.   cm.
    "A Fireside book."
    Includes index.
    ISBN 0-671-68720-4
    1. Bathrooms–Remodeling–Amateurs' manuals.   2. Bedrooms–
Remodeling–Amateurs' manuals.   3. Dwellings–Remodeling–Amateurs'
manuals.   I. Johnson, Hugh.   II. Title.   III. Title: Do-it-yourself
with style.
TH4816.3.B43C66   1989
643'.53--dc20
                                                              89-10106
                                                                  CIP

The publisher would like to thank the following companies
for supplying material for photography:

18 Ideal Standard Ltd, C P Hart Ltd, The Conran Shop; **31**
Ideal Standard Ltd, London Architectural Salvage
Company, The Conran Shop; **36** Paul Jones, Eximious
Ltd, Sam Walker; **64** Gallery of Antique Costume and
Textiles, The Conran Shop.

Project Editor JOANNA BRADSHAW
Assistant Editor SIMON WILLIS
Copy Editor RICHARD DAWES
U.S. Consultants RAY PORFILIO, MILES HERTER

Art Editor MERYL LLOYD
Design Assistant ALISON SHACKLETON
Illustrator PAUL BRYANT
Visualizer JEAN MORLEY

Photographer HUGH JOHNSON
Photographic Stylist CLAIRE LLOYD
Photographic Assistants SIMON LEE, PETER WILLETT

Picture Research NADINE BAZAR
Production SHANE LASK, SONYA SIBBONS

PUBLISHER'S ACKNOWLEDGMENTS
The publisher would like to thank the following for their
invaluable assistance in producing this book:

The Conran Studios, Julie Drake, Rebecca Verrill,
Malcolm Harold and all at Benchmark Woodworking
Limited, Tabby Riley, and Alex Wilcock.

The projects in this book were specially built by SEAN SUTCLIFFE
of Benchmark Woodworking Limited.

Special thanks to PAUL BRYANT for his superb original illustrations.

PLEASE NOTE
Before embarking on any major building work on your home,
you should check the law concerning building regulations and
planning. It is also important to obtain specialist advice
on plumbing, gas, and electricity, before attempting any
alterations to these services yourself.

While we have made every effort to ensure that all the
information contained in this book is correct, the publisher
cannot be held responsible for any loss, damage, or injury
caused by reliance on such information.

DIMENSIONS
Do not mix imperial and metric when you are making a calculation.

Typeset by Servis Filmsetting Limited
Printed and bound in Italy by Amilcare Pizzi SpA

CONTENTS

INTRODUCTION

The bathroom is not a simple room to renovate, restore, or
redecorate. Often, a new bathroom seems to be an expensive
luxury when compared with other home improvements which
appear more urgent. Besides, any undertaking in the bathroom
can turn into a major task if new plumbing is involved.
However, as the hand-built bathroom and other projects
featured in this book show, remodeling the bathroom can be as
easy and satisfying to carry out as work in any other room.
Leaving the bathtub, basin, shower, and lavatory in place, you
can completely transform your bathroom by tiling walls, by
laying a new floor, and by adding shelves and cabinets, towel
rods and mirrors to your existing layout.

In the bedroom, doing-it-yourself gives you the opportunity
to create clothes storage that meets your exact requirements.
You can make the room more comfortable and practical by
constructing your own built-in wardrobes, building a bed, or
even creating a work area. A folding screen can quickly and
efficiently modify a spare room from a study or a place for
storage to a cozy guest bedroom.

Terence Conran.

BATHROOM MATERIALS

The bathroom should, of necessity, be a room of resistant, durable surfaces. Marble, mirror, slate, glass, laminate, chrome, plastic, vitreous china, treated wood, and water-resistant paint are the tough, elegant materials that bathrooms are made of. Softness can be provided by towels, bathrobes, comfortable easy chairs, cotton shower curtains, and bath mats.

Soften a bathroom considerably with accessories, or turn it into a stark interior—the level of sleek functionalism is up to you. For example, if you decide to tile the room, the type of tiles you choose can have dramatically different effects. Brick-shaped tiles in white ceramic with a border of a contrasting dark color produce an old-fashioned and traditional appeal. Expensive marble slips are a pure luxury; decorated or textured tiles will have their own impact, while plain white squares will provide a simple harmony.

The materials you choose will depend largely on your budget. Marble or granite is not easily affordable or simple to install. Tiles are also a relatively expensive way to decorate large areas, although not difficult to apply if the wall surface is flat. Wooden paneling can be highly effective and is available by the yard. Tiles can be used for areas where water will often be splashed, and other wall surfaces can be painted with water-resistant paint.

Floor coverings must be practical, resilient, and preferably waterproof. The drawback to using ceramic or marble tiles, or other hard surfaces, for flooring is that they are cold, whereas sealed cork and inexpensive sheet vinyl provide warmth. Carpet is best avoided, but rugs, especially if made from washable cotton, are a good alternative. Any bathroom floor should be able to withstand dampness; vinyl tiles and wood block will rise easily if water penetrates the surface, so carefully choose your flooring.

MIXING MATERIALS

Small white tiles, a clear plastic shower curtain, and a pretty porthole window (above) create a bright, airy bathroom in a small space.

Exposed brick forms a partition wall between bedroom and bathroom (center). The strong texture of the brick is offset against the clean and smooth white tiles.

Glass bricks are an excellent choice for a bathroom (below) as they are easily wiped clean and allow light to shine through them. Here they have been effectively combined with a steel sink with exposed pipes and a dramatic black Venetian blind.

DECORATIVE FINISHES

A showerhead has been recessed into marble slips above a bathtub (opposite left) and a deep alcove allows for generous shelves. The elements of the bathroom are unified by the pale gray marble to stylish effect.

Black and white tiles form a decorative checkerboard frieze (opposite above right) in this lively bathroom. The black slats on the white blinds continue the duotone theme. Other strong features include the chrome supports for the double basins and the "dressing room" lights around the mirror.

Unusual finishes give this bathroom originality (opposite right center). The basin unit is made from black-stained wood, and is topped with marble-chip terrazzo to produce a dramatic and luxurious effect.

The rolled top of an old-fashioned bathtub (opposite below right) and the traditional contrasting strip of tiles at "picture rail" height set the scene for a bathroom styled in the past. A basin has been set into an old wood cabinet and the mirror has a wooden frame.

BATHROOM STORAGE

What you keep in the bathroom apart from essential items depends upon the size of the room. A large bathroom can accommodate a spacious closet, which you can build yourself, for storing linen, towels, bulk supplies of toilet paper, and anything else you want out of the way. A tiny bathroom should be more minimal, with just the fixtures and sufficient supplies of toiletries in evidence. Towels and bulk supplies can be stored elsewhere.

Closed closets and open shelves are the ideal combination for bathroom storage. Open shelves can carry jars, flowers, towels, and other objects, but remember that whatever you display in a bathroom has to be regularly washed and dusted. It is easy to be seduced into displaying rows of pretty bottles and lotions as seen in endless magazine articles, but in reality a relatively bare bathroom is much more practical. The area above the basin and the shelf around the bathtub is the favorite place for such displays. When planning yours, take into account which items you need close by and which would look better behind closed doors; build your units accordingly.

On open shelves, store items neatly in containers. Large wicker baskets can add an attractive and softening dimension to a white-tiled bathroom.

Shelves may be tiled if they are built as chunky hollow constructions rather than made of single planks of wood. Glass shelves are always well-suited to bathrooms. You can create a unit incorporating glass shelves in the design so that they rest within a frame of wood. Cabinets are also reasonably easy to construct and can have mirrored or painted doors.

Design the whole area above the basin with care, taking into account the amount of display space you want and how much hidden storage you need there. If you have children, you should store razors and medicines in a lockable cabinet that is out of reach of tiny hands.

A built-in cupboard can be extremely useful. In a limited space, closet-space can be part of a vanity unit but in a larger bathroom, design a closet to fill an entire wall. Doors can be made of wooden louver slats or painted MDF (medium-density fiberboard), they can be laminated or glazed. Either of the wardrobe designs illustrated on pages 36 and 54 can be adapted for the bathroom.

If kitchen space is limited, washing machines and clothes dryers can be installed in the bathroom, but make sure there is adequate ventilation and that the machines can be easily reached for maintenance. In some instances, it is illegal to install washing machines in the bathroom, so check local codes first.

The area of exposed pipes behind a toilet can be attractively concealed behind a wooden housing which will also provide a useful shelf along the top. If you have a bidet, this can be installed in a similar way for a neat appearance. Whenever you box-in pipes, always consider turning the wooden box itself into something useful such as a shelf or even a seat.

If you are building your own bathtub surround, consider incorporating a hinged shelf if there is room at the end of the tub, so that the otherwise dead space beneath can be used for storage.

Soiled clothes and linen are often kept in an overflowing and rather untidy basket or plastic container which does nothing to enhance a bathroom. If you are creating your own bathroom, consider building a box for dirty linen. In an existing bathroom, one could be incorporated into a cupboard. A broad shelf could have a boxed-in support and be hinged along its length, or in part, to act as a lid; in addition, you could turn the lid into a seat using a loose cushion.

BATHROOM STORAGE
This vanity unit is styled for storage (top) with its practical drawers and cupboards.

In a high but narrow Edwardian bathroom (above), the dead space near the ceiling has been used for pine storage closets, housed in a false wall.

A glossy stylized bathroom (opposite) has ceramic-tiled, steel-faced partitions to hold glass shelves. Further storage is provided on metal carts which are pushed into the recess when they are not in use.

Given adequate storage space, the bathroom is an excellent location for a spacious, fully fitted closet when you require extra storage. This elegant fitted unit (opposite above right) is given a graphic black trim.

The area around the basin is easily utilized for extra storage (opposite below right). Here the closets are situated above and below the basin to hide bathroom clutter.

BEDROOM POTENTIAL

The bedroom is a private haven for relaxation and sleep. Here you can concentrate on building projects which will heighten your enjoyment of the room and enhance it.

There are still practical considerations to think about before starting work – clothes storage, lighting, and comfort are all important factors – but what you put in your bedroom, and the style you create there, is completely up to you. There is enormous potential here and doing-it-yourself can make all the difference between an untidy, uncomfortable, and unrelaxing room and a well-appointed, stylish, and appealing one.

Wardrobes are an obvious and worthwhile project to undertake, since good fitted storage will add enormously to the tidiness and convenience of the room. They can also vastly improve its appearance. By designing and building them yourself you can ensure that they fit the dimensions of the room precisely and are in keeping with its decorative scheme and architectural details.

There are many other things to build in the bedroom. Window seats are a delightful addition if you want somewhere to read and relax, have a room with a view, and need some extra storage, since the area below the seat provides capacity for bedding, linen, and clothes.

Of course, you can also build a bed. There is a spectacular bed project with spacious built-in storage later in this book, but a simpler model could be created instead. A platform for a mattress is all you need. It could be a platform under which you can stand in order to make the best use of very limited space. Below it you can create a storage area, install a desk, open shelves, or a second bunk bed.

You can embellish a hand-made or store-bought bed in many ways. Add a headboard as something to rest against, as a decorative feature, and as protection for the wall behind. A simple frame with four posts, one at each corner of the bed, connected at the top, will transform any simple divan into a magnificent and luxurious four poster.

The materials you use in the bedroom are not going to have to endure too much wear and tear so it is here that you can indulge yourself with more expensive materials; they will not need to be replaced as often as those used elsewhere. Natural wood or painted cheaper wood is always effective. In small bedrooms, mirror can be used for door fronts to increase the sense of space.

SEATING SOLUTIONS

The broad sweep of a bay window (opposite above) has been turned into a sunny place to sit with an easily-constructed wooden window seat. Low level radiators fit below the center seat. In a smaller bedroom (opposite below right) a padded window seat has filled the gentle curve of a bay window.

In the narrow corner of a bedroom (below center), a television has been placed on an angled bracket above a built-in storage box. Plump cushions on top turn it into a seat.

INSPIRING IDEAS

Romantic muslin drapes (below left) are hung above a bed from wooden poles bound together and suspended from the ceiling by chains.

A flat-fronted, wall-to-wall fitted wardrobe has been given glamorous mirror doors (below right). The wall of glass reflects and doubles any light source in the room, adds depth and space, and is stunning in a room which is dedicated as much to dressing as to sleeping.

Dramatic decorative detailing has been added to a bedroom (opposite below left) by uplighters placed on columns. These highlight a curved architrave which frames a door. On either side are fitted wardrobes.

Providing practical bedside shelves, a unit in mellow wood (opposite below center) has been built at the head of a bed, situated beneath an attractive sloping window. The wide shelf which sits on top of the unit offers display space and the lower shelves can carry books, radio, lights, and other essentials.

BEDROOM STORAGE

Clothes are the major item for storage in bedrooms. You may also want rows of bookshelves, a linen chest, a vanity-unit for make-up and toiletries, a display area for a treasured collection, or a corner fitted as a home office. These are, however, added extras. We all have to store clothes. A dressing room is undoubtedly the best solution but one that is only possible with adequate space.

Doing-it-yourself not only allows you the freedom to design and build a fine wardrobe in keeping with the room but also to customize it to meet your individual needs. You can decide the length of shoe rails, the depth and number of drawers for underwear, accessories, socks, and scarves, the length of a closet pole for bulkier garments, and the number of shelves and how they should be divided for sweaters, t-shirts, and jeans.

There are many ready-made storage accessories for fitting out cupboards, and some of the most effective are made from wire mesh and plastic; they include drawers and containers. Alternatively you can construct fixtures from wood. Attach mirrors to the inside doors of wardrobes so that you can check your appearance. Visit a few stores which you consider to be well-designed, see how they display

Linking a bedroom with a bathroom (above) is a passage which has been transformed into a walk-in wardrobe with ingenious wooden fixtures.

A false wall has created a deep and beautifully detailed recess for a window and allowed for low subtle closets to be added on either side (center).

their clothes, and use this as inspiration to design your changing room.

A dressing room or dressing area can be made even in quite limited space by building a partition in the bedroom, utilizing a passage, or using a box room. Line it from top to bottom with pigeon-holes, rails, shelves, and drawers to create a neat, orderly storage area.

You can incorporate lighting into a wardrobe or as part of the dressing room by installing it under shelves. In addition, make sure you have adequate light in front of the mirror.

Low closets or high shelves can be equally effective in a bedroom – as discreet storage or display areas for any kind of item from linen and towels to personal mementoes.

In a very small bedroom, a studio room for living in, or a box room for guests, built-in storage is particularly important. Use every spare inch of space to the best possible advantage, filling whole walls with shelves and cupboards, building units rather than using freestanding wardrobes or tables. Make the bed into a storage area by choosing a mattress or divan that can be placed on a storage platform. Place shelves above or below the bed rather than use bedside tables.

A magnificent built-in wardrobe, everybody's dream (below and opposite), is fitted with superb clothes storage – a closet pole, suspended open drawers, and neat shelves. The folding doors are faced with mirror.

TILED BATHROOM

Traditionally, bathrooms tend to be rather badly organized rooms, in which a collection of pipework and bathroom equipment is arranged, so it seems, to suit the convenience of the plumber rather than the bather.

This design tries to organize the various elements of a bathroom so that plumbing work, which can often look rather brutal, is hidden from view. The bathroom is uncluttered and easy to clean – requirements which I think are essential, given that the whole point of a bathroom is hygiene.

The bathroom system is remarkably easy to construct once you have mastered the simple art of cutting, laying, and grouting wall tiles. The cavity behind the bathtub, shower, and washbasin allows for pipework and drainage to be hidden. The large mirror behind the bathtub, while not essential, gives a sense of scale to a small space.

Tile colors and patterns can obviously be selected to suit your own particular preferences. I think that plain white tiles combined with white baths, basins, bidets, and showers are particularly pleasant in bathrooms; they have light, reflective qualities, that induce an atmosphere of cleanliness and hygiene.

Tiled frame for a simple vanity unit

Mirror

light under tiled shelf

Recessed Basin in tiled top, with wood shelf & towel rod.

FRONT ELEVATION

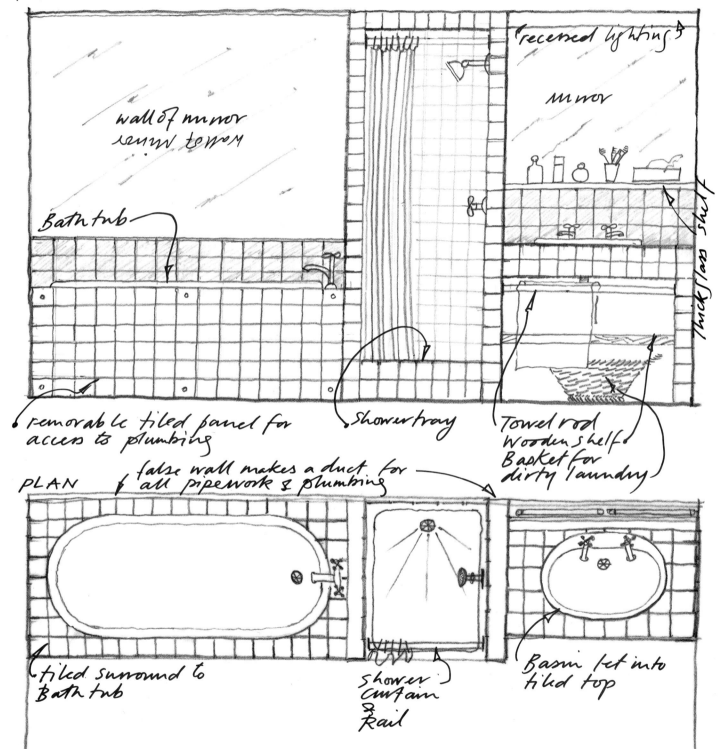

wall of mirror

recessed lighting

mirror

Bath tub

Thick glass shelf

removable tiled panel for access to plumbing

Shower tray

Towel rod
Wooden shelf
Basket for dirty laundry

PLAN

false wall makes a duct for all pipework & plumbing

tiled surround to Bath tub

shower curtain & Rail

Basin let into tiled top

TILED BATHROOM: BATHTUB UNIT

This project shows how to make a tiled bathroom with the fixtures set into hollow panel frames so that all the pipework is kept out of sight. The dimensions of the frames are based on those of your bathroom suite and your wall tiles. Obviously, the layout will have to be adapted to suit your particular bathroom.

It is strongly advised that you make a sketch of the proposed bathroom and discuss it with your plumber and electrician so that they can suggest the exact positioning of pipes and wiring, where access will be needed, and the sequence in which the work will be carried out. Coordinating your tasks with the installation of the plumbing and wiring will have to be carefully worked out between the three of you, since it is easier to put in the pipes and cables as the elements of the bathroom are built. Of course, this is not a problem if you are doing your own plumbing. This is now feasible, thanks to the availability of a wide range of easy-to-fit modern plumbing components, such as plastic supply and waste pipes, and push-fit joints. However, by building the frames and fitting some of the panels temporarily, it should be possible to do all the plumbing in one session.

Before starting, it is important to spend some time working out the dimensions carefully so that the minimum of tiles will need to be cut, and so that any cut tiles can be located where they will be least noticeable. Try to use only whole tiles. Tiles which overlap the edges of others should be positioned so that their flat surface is uppermost and the joint is at the side. This will occur at the top of the shower tray and where the bath and wall tiles come on to the bathtub. Always think about how water will run off the tiles. Wherever possible it should not run down into a joint, but off one tile and on to another to avoid unnecessary water penetration.

TOOLS

STEEL MEASURING TAPE

CARPENTER'S LEVEL

TRY SQUARE

UTILITY KNIFE and MARKING GAUGE (useful but not essential)

CIRCULAR POWER SAW (or small hand saw)

BACK SAW

POWER SABER SAW (or compass saw)

DRILL (hand or power)

TWIST DRILL BITS
$\frac{1}{8}$in (3mm) for pilot holes
$\frac{3}{16}$in (5mm) for clearance holes

MASONRY DRILL BIT to suit anchors being used

COUNTERSINK BIT

COLD CHISEL

SMOOTHING PLANE

ROUTER and ROUTER BIT

PLUMB BOB and CHALK

SCREWDRIVER

HAMMER

NAILSET

POWER FINISHING SANDER (or hand-sanding block)

TILING TOOLS

CAULKING GUN (if required)

METAL DETECTOR

MATERIALS

Part	Quantity	Material	Length
BATHTUB FRAME			
TOP AND BOTTOM RAILS	4	2 × 3in (50 × 75mm) S4S softwood	Bathtub length, plus width of two tiles
UPRIGHT RAILS	8	2 × 3in (50 × 75mm) S4S softwood	Internal distance between top and bottom rails
END FRAME TOP AND BOTTOM RAILS	4	2 × 3in (50 × 75mm) S4S softwood	Internal distance between inside faces of front and back panels
END FRAME UPRIGHT RAILS	4	2 × 3in (50 × 75mm) S4S softwood	Internal distance between end frame top and bottom rails
END SHELVING STRIPS	2	$\frac{1}{2}$in (12mm) water-resistant plywood; cut to tile width	Distance from back wall to front face of bath panel
BACK SHELVING STRIP	1	Plywood as above; width as above	Length of bathtub
FRONT SHELVING STRIP	1	Plywood as above; cut to tile width, less a tile thickness to allow shelf tiles to overlap edge of facing tiles on bathtub panel	Length of bathtub
BATHTUB PANEL	1	Plywood as above; width as height of front frame	As front frame and to overlap end panels (if any)

The entire framework is made from 2 × 3in (50 × 75mm) S4S (smooth 4 sides) softwood, skinned with $\frac{3}{4}$in (19mm) or $\frac{1}{2}$in (12mm) water-resistant plywood. Our tiles are $4\frac{1}{4}$in (108mm) square, which works well with this framework.

BATHTUB

Measure for the frames to fit each side of the bathtub, allowing for $\frac{1}{2}$in (12mm) plywood to be attached on top. This will be exactly level with the rim of the bathtub, and will allow the tiles to rest on the tub rim for an easily sealed joint.

Using 2 × 3in (50 × 75mm) lumber, nail the frames so that the top and bottom rails run the full length of the bathtub recess and the uprights fit between them – one at each end and two spaced inside them at equal distances.

The bathtub will either rest in a cradle or will be supplied with adjustable legs. The manufacturer's assembly instructions should be carefully followed. To spread the load across several floor joists, the bathtub feet should be rested on 2 × 3in (50 × 75mm) battens laid on their sides on the floor, and allowance should be made for these when measuring the height of the tub. The bathtub should be carefully positioned lengthwise and widthwise to ensure that water drains properly to the waste outlet.

BATHTUB FRAME ASSEMBLY

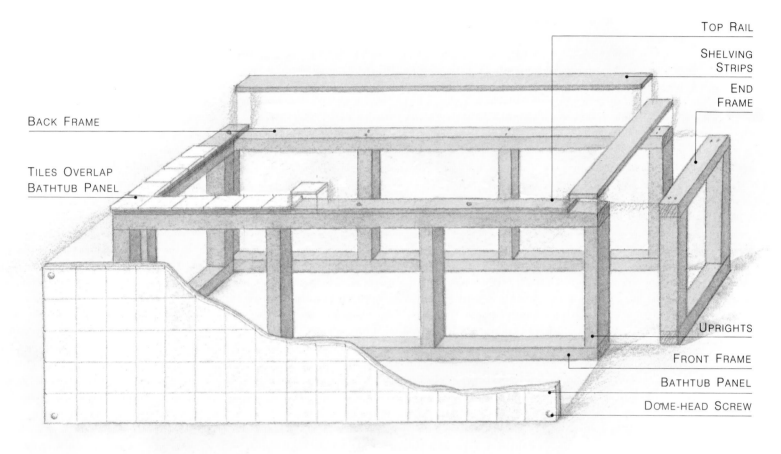

TOP RAIL

SHELVING STRIPS

END FRAME

BACK FRAME

TILES OVERLAP BATHTUB PANEL

UPRIGHTS

FRONT FRAME

BATHTUB PANEL

DOME-HEAD SCREW

End frames are made up in the same way as the front and back frames, and are made to fit between them. Allowance is made for the thickness of the front panel ($\frac{1}{2}$in [12mm]). If you are installing the bathtub tight to the wall or partitions at the foot or head, these end frames can be dispensed with, although you will need to cut top rails at the ends to support the shelving strips.

INSTALLING FRAMES

Screw the back frame to the wall, shimming underneath it if necessary to ensure that it is level. Screw through the end frames into the back frame uprights and into the wall or partition at each end if there is one there. Put the bathtub in place and level it for correct drainage.

Position the front frame, screwing it into the end frames and the side walls or partitions where appropriate.

ATTACHING THE PLYWOOD SHELF STRIPS

Measure for these strips using $4\frac{1}{4}$in (108mm) wide (or tile width if different) $\frac{1}{2}$in (12mm) water-resistant plywood to the width of the frame to the outer edges of the front frame, so that they fit across the bathtub at the head and foot, overhanging on the inside edges of the top rail.

Measure the spaces along the sides of the frame between the end shelves and cut two more lengths of plywood to fit between them. Note that the front shelf will be slightly narrower than the others as the tiles on this shelf will overlap the edges of the tiles used to cover the front panel of the bathtub unit.

Apply clear silicone-rubber caulking to the inside edges of all of the shelves and screw them down into the frame on all sides so that the plywood butts against the bathtub exactly level with the rim. The join between the bathtub and the shelves must be sealed with caulking to prevent water getting under the edging tiles. These strips make a good surface for tiling.

INSTALLING FRONT PANEL

Cut out the front panel from $\frac{1}{2}$in (12mm) water-resistant plywood and fit it over the frame and any end panels, if required. The front panel must be removable to make access easy in case you need to adjust or repair the internal plumbing. The panel is secured with dome-head screws inserted through the tiles once these have been fitted.

TILED BATHROOM: SHOWER UNIT

MATERIALS

Part	Quantity	Material	Length
SHOWER PARTITION			
FRONT STUD	1	2 × 3in (50 × 75mm) S4S softwood	Floor to ceiling height
TOP AND BOTTOM RAILS	2 per side	2 × 3in (50 × 75mm) S4S softwood	Back of front stud to back wall
BACK STUD	1	2 × 3in (50 × 75mm) S4S softwood	Internal distance between top and bottom rails
MIDDLE RAILS	As required	2 × 3in (50 × 75mm) S4S softwood	Internal distance between front and back studs
SIDE PANELS	2 per side	¾in (19mm) water-resistant plywood	Length and width as overall dimensions of lumber partition frame
SHOWER BASE			
TOP AND BOTTOM RAILS	4	2 × 2in (50 × 50mm) S4S softwood	Width between side partitions
SIDE STUDS	4	2 × 2in (50 × 50mm) S4S softwood	Height of shower tray, less 4½in (112mm)*
FRONT PANEL	1	¾in (19mm) water-resistant plywood; width as distance between side panels	Height of base frame
TOP PANEL	1	As above; width as above	Width from front of base panel to shower tray
SHOWER CEILING			
CEILING PANEL	1	¾in (19mm) water-resistant plywood; depth as width of recess	Depth of shower recess
FRONT PANEL	1	As above; depth as above	Height of tiles
FRONT PANEL SUPPORT RAIL	1	2 × 2in (50 × 50mm) S4S softwood	Width of ceiling panel
CEILING FIXING BATTENS	2	2 × 2in (50 × 50mm) S4S softwood	Depth of ceiling panel, less 2in (50mm)*

*Approximate lengths only – refer to copy for actual size

SHOWER PARTITIONS

Measure the floor-to-ceiling height for the front stud in exactly the place where it will be positioned. Then measure for the top and bottom rails to be positioned behind the front stud, having previously worked out the front-to-back depth of your shower recess (dependent on size of shower tray – ours is the depth of the tray plus one tile height). Cut them to length from the 2 × 3in (50 × 75mm) S4S lumber. Next, cut the back stud to fit between the top and bottom rails, that is, to the length of the front stud, less the combined thickness of the top and bottom rails (approximately 3in [75mm]).

BASIC FRAME

Nail the front stud on to the top rail with 10d common nails, driving them in with a support behind (see **Techniques, page 84**). Nail the bottom rail in place at the bottom, then insert the back stud ½in (12mm) in from the ends, to make scribing easier when the partitions are attached to the wall. (If pipes have to be run along the back, this back stud can be positioned even farther in.) Nail the back stud in place. Repeat the process for a second partition, if one is required.

MIDDLE RAILS

These brace the basic frame to make it sturdier, and are also used to make attachments to any adjacent support battens and fixtures. They should therefore be placed at heights which coincide with the locations of these fixtures, such as faucets and shower heads.

In our case, a rail is needed where the basin and shelf supports meet the side. You may need additional support for the shower spray head, depending on the type of shower used (fig 1, page 24). Another cross rail would be needed where you have to make any joints in the plywood panels to make up the full height of your room. Space other cross-rails at intervals of about 24–36in (610–900mm).

It is a good idea to include a small removable access panel opposite the shower fixtures in case there is

1 Assembly of the Shower Partition Basic Frame
Assemble basic framework from S4S lumber as shown, using common nails. Nail front stud to top rail, then bottom rail, and add the back stud, insetting it by ½in (12mm) to aid scribing.

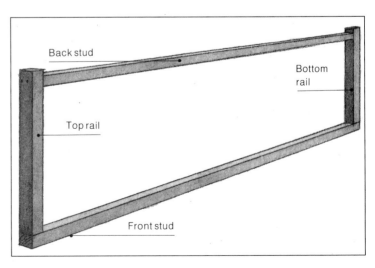

SHOWER UNIT ASSEMBLY

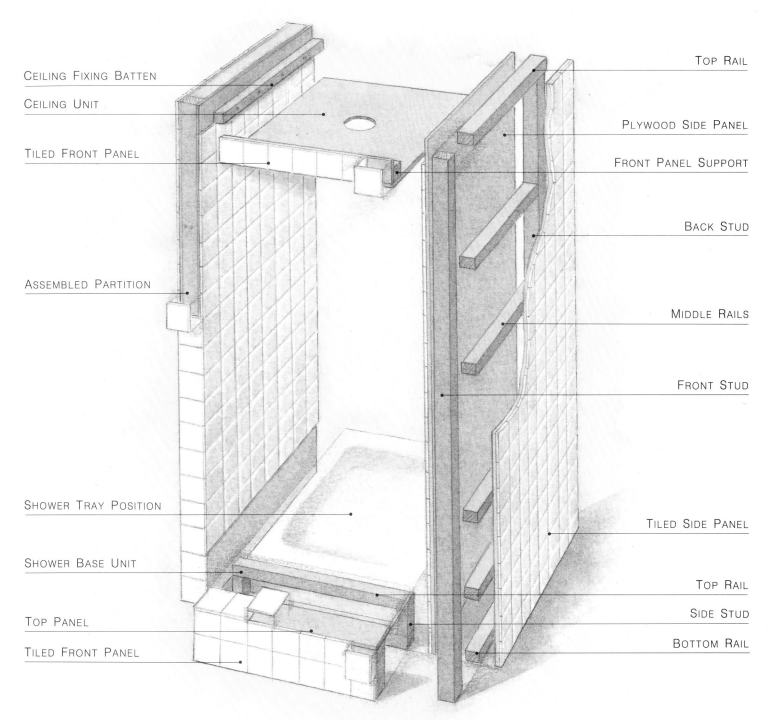

CEILING FIXING BATTEN

CEILING UNIT

TILED FRONT PANEL

ASSEMBLED PARTITION

SHOWER TRAY POSITION

SHOWER BASE UNIT

TOP PANEL

TILED FRONT PANEL

TOP RAIL

PLYWOOD SIDE PANEL

FRONT PANEL SUPPORT

BACK STUD

MIDDLE RAILS

FRONT STUD

TILED SIDE PANEL

TOP RAIL

SIDE STUD

BOTTOM RAIL

TILED BATHROOM: SHOWER UNIT

ever a problem with the plumbing. This is done by making a panel to coincide with whole tiles (fig 2). The panel is attached to additional rails inside the frame. You may prefer to make one large panel to give access to the shower mixing valve and the spray head. If you are using a plumber, ask his advice.

ADDING THE SIDES

When both frames are nailed up, measure for the side panels to finish flush with all the edges. Then cut out the required number of panels from ¾in (19mm) water-resistant plywood, making sure that you cut them all square. Mark the center lines of all the studs on the edges of the frames as a guide for nailing the side panels.

Lay the frame flat and lay the *inner* plywood panel on top. Line up the edge of the panel accurately with the *front* stud. Glue together and then nail down into the stud about every 6in (150mm), using 4d common nails. Use the center marks on the edges of the frame as an accurate guide for the nail positions,

to ensure that they are driven centrally into the rails.

Having nailed the front stud, pull the rest of the frame into square to align with the other edges of the plywood. Mark on the face of the plywood the center lines of the rails and back stud so that you have guide lines for nailing.

Continue nailing down along the top and bottom rails, the back stud, and the middle rails, checking as you do so that the frame is still square. Do not install the other side panel at this stage.

Repeat for the other partition.

INSTALLING PARTITIONS

Put the partitions in place, spacing them by the width of the shower tray. Use a carpenter's level and plumb bob to check that the partitions are standing plumb. Do any scribing necessary to fit the partitions to the wall (see **Techniques, page 91**). This does not have to be very accurate as the final joint between the partition and the wall will be achieved with the tiles. Install the partitions by screwing through the

back stud and shimming any gaps between the back stud and the wall where the screws are positioned.

Screw through the top rail into the ceiling. If possible, screw into the ceiling joists. You can find these by using a metal detector to locate the nails securing them (see **Techniques, page 84**). If the partitions fall between two joists (as is likely where the partitions run parallel with them), secure a blocking of 2 × 3in (50 × 75mm) lumber between the joists and screw into this. Depending on the location of your bathroom, you may have to go into the attic to do this, or it may be necessary to lift a few floorboards in the room above the shower position. It is a good idea to get an electrician to install the ceiling light at the same time.

Finally, screw the bottom rail into the floor, shimming under it if necessary to ensure that it sits square.

Temporarily attach the other plywood panel with a few nails only, not fully driven home. This will allow easy removal later, during plumbing, and will allow you to finish your framework first.

SHOWER BASE

Put the shower tray in place temporarily and adjust its legs so that the top of the tray is the height of whole tiles. Make a frame for the "step" at the front from 2 × 2in (50 × 50mm) S4S lumber to the width of the recess by the height of the shower tray, but allowing for the thickness of the plywood panel (¾in [19mm]) which rests on top. The rails run the full width between the partitions, with the uprights between them. Butt the panel to the front of the shower tray and screw through the uprights into the sides of the partitions.

Make up an identical frame to the first, to be positioned in from the front edge of the partition by the thickness of the plywood. Screw through the uprights into the side partitions as before. If, as in our case, the total width of the step is only one tile, the two frames will almost touch each other. Cut a piece of ¾in (19mm) plywood to fit the front of this frame, flush with the top edge. Cut a top piece to rest on top of the frame, flush with the front of the

① Adding Sides to Frames
Middle rails are required at fixing positions for the bathtub or basin unit, possibly for the shower fixture, and also where it is necessary to join plywood panels. Nail down every 6in (150mm).

② Installing an Access Panel
It is wise to include an access panel opposite the shower fixture. Panel should coincide with whole tiles.

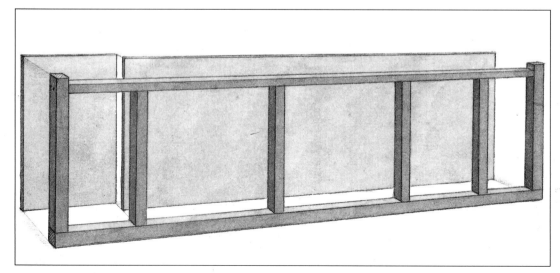

frame and butting up to the shower tray. Do not fit these pieces yet, so that you will have access for fitting the shower tray and installing the pipework (see **Plumbing and Wiring, page 28**).

Refer to the manufacturer's instructions on how to assemble and install the shower tray. Some trays have to be rested on sturdy lumber battens to spread the weight of the tray when it is in use: if this is the case with yours, you may have to adjust the height of the support legs to accommodate the thickness of the support battens.

When attaching bathroom fixtures into the lumber frame, use a caulking gun to insert a generous line of caulking between the fixture and the framework. This acts as a second line of defense should water get under the tiles owing to the breakdown of the caulking which will be used between the fitting and the tiles (see **Tiling, page 94**).

SHOWER CEILING

Measure the recess in the shower area and cut out a ceiling panel from ¾in (19mm) water-resistant plywood. Cut a front panel to rest on top of it, so that the total depth is sufficient to house a shower downlighter, while the panel lines up with a joint line in the tiled partitions and the wall. It is best to work out exactly where the tiles will lie. Alternatively, tile the partitions up to where you require the ceiling. Make up the ceiling unit and continue tiling.

Use a 2 × 2in (50 × 50mm) batten, glued and screwed in place, to join the ceiling panel and the front panel together at right angles. Assuming it is safe, cut a hole in the middle of the ceiling panel, and install the downlighter according to the manufacturer's instructions.

Cut two lengths of 2 × 2in (50 × 50mm) lumber to be attached horizontally to the inside faces of the partition panels, to allow the ceiling unit to be attached to the sides. Cut these battens so that they will fit behind the front batten, but do not secure them or the ceiling unit yet, as the plumbing must be completed.

Buy a shower rail the width of the shower recess and screw in place.

③ Making Shower Base to Height of Shower Tray
The base comprises two frames, covered by a front panel and joined by a top panel which is cut to the width of one tile. If shower tray is only one tile height high, top and bottom rails of frame will almost touch.

④ Shower Ceiling Assembly
Cut ceiling panel to fit between partitions. Front panel must be deep enough to hide shower downlighter.

GLASS SHELF
A sleek glass shelf sits above the basin unit (see page 29 for instructions).

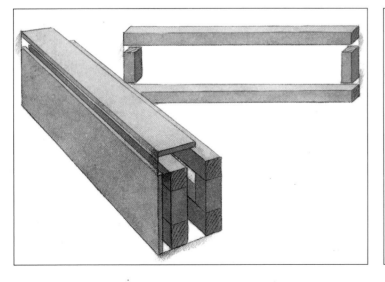

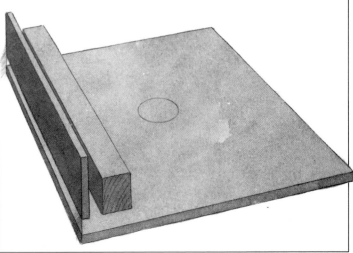

TILED BATHROOM: BASIN UNIT

MATERIALS

Part	Quantity	Material	Length
BASIN FRAME			
PARTITION FRAME FRONT STUD	1	2 × 3in (50 × 75mm) S4S softwood	Height of basin, less $\frac{1}{2}$in (12mm)
TOP AND BOTTOM RAILS	2	2 × 3in (50 × 75mm) S4S softwood	Distance from inside face of front stud to back wall
BACK STUD	1	2 × 3in (50 × 75mm) S4S softwood	Height of basin, less $\frac{1}{2}$in (12mm), less 4in (100mm)*
MIDDLE RAIL	1	2 × 3in (50 × 75mm) S4S softwood	Distance between inside faces of front and back studs
SIDE PANELS	1 or 2	$\frac{3}{4}$in (19mm) water-resistant plywood; width as overall width of frame	Height of frame
FRONT PANEL	1	Plywood as above; width to give sufficient depth to hide underside of basin	Distance between partition panel and side of shower partition
TOP PANEL	1	$\frac{3}{4}$in (19mm) water-resistant plywood; width as depth of recess	Width of alcove
FRONT PANEL SUPPORT RAIL	1	2 × 3in (50 × 75mm) S4S softwood or 2 × 2in (50 × 50mm) S4S softwood	Width of alcove
BASIN SUPPORT BATTEN	1	2 × 2in (50 × 50mm) S4S softwood	As top rail of basin partition frame
UNDER-BASIN SHELF PANEL	1	$\frac{1}{2}$in (12mm) laminated particleboard (or plywood if to be tiled); width as depth of recess, less about 5in (125mm)	Distance between inside faces (after tiling) of shower and basin support partitions
EDGE BANDING	1	1 × 2in (25 × 50mm) pine	As above
SHELF-SUPPORT BATTENS	2	1 × 1in (25 × 25mm) S4S softwood	As width of under-basin shelf panel
GLASS SHELF	1	Tempered glass as recommended by supplier. Width as required, plus $\frac{1}{2}$in (12mm) to be inset in rear-wall plaster	Width of basin alcove, plus 1in (25mm)
REAR-WALL GLASS SHELF-SUPPORT BATTEN	1	$\frac{1}{2} \times \frac{1}{2}$in (12 × 12mm) hardwood (or as plaster thickness)	Width of basin alcove, plus 1in (25mm)
SIDE-WALL GLASS SHELF-SUPPORT BATTEN	2	$\frac{1}{2}$in × $\frac{1}{2}$in (12 × 12mm) hardwood (or as plaster thickness)	Width of glass shelf, less $\frac{1}{2}$in (12mm) (or batten thickness, if different)
VALANCE PANEL	1	$\frac{3}{4}$in (19mm) plywood; width as tile depth	Width of basin alcove
VALANCE SUPPORT BLOCKS	2	1 × 2in (25 × 50mm) S4S softwood	As valance depth, less 1in (25mm)

*Approximate length only – refer to copy for actual size

BASIN

The basin is set into a tiled surface with a shelf underneath. The frame is installed between the shower partition and another low-level partition. Alternatively, you can make the fitting between two low-level ones.

BASIN PARTITION

Work out how high you want your basin, and how far out from the wall you want to extend, allowing a generous space around the basin.

Make up the partition frame in the same way as for the shower, but only one middle rail will be required. This will be at the level you want to attach the shelf supports. Note this level as you will need to know where it is once the sides are in place.

Mark the center line of all the rails and studs on the edges of the frame as before, as a guide for nailing on the side panels. Cut these out. If the partition is to be attached to a wall it will need only one side panel. Do not install it at this stage. If it is *not* going against a wall, attach only the outer one (the farthest from the basin) by following the procedure described for the shower partition on page 22 (attach the front stud first, and pull it into square to complete nailing). Secure the partition panel in place as described above.

If the partition is to be attached to a wall, stand the framework $\frac{1}{2}$in (12mm) away from the wall, checking that it is plumb, and shimming the bottom rail level if necessary. Use shims between the frame and the wall at the point where the screws go in. If the distance between the frame and the wall varies because the wall is uneven, make the $\frac{1}{2}$in (12mm) gap between the frame and the wall the maximum width. This will avoid any need for scribing to fit the frame to the wall, and will still allow for whole tiles to fit the front edge of the partition. Fit the inner side panel in place and temporarily nail to frame.

Sawing 81
Nailing 84
Finding verticals 92

BASIN UNIT ASSEMBLY

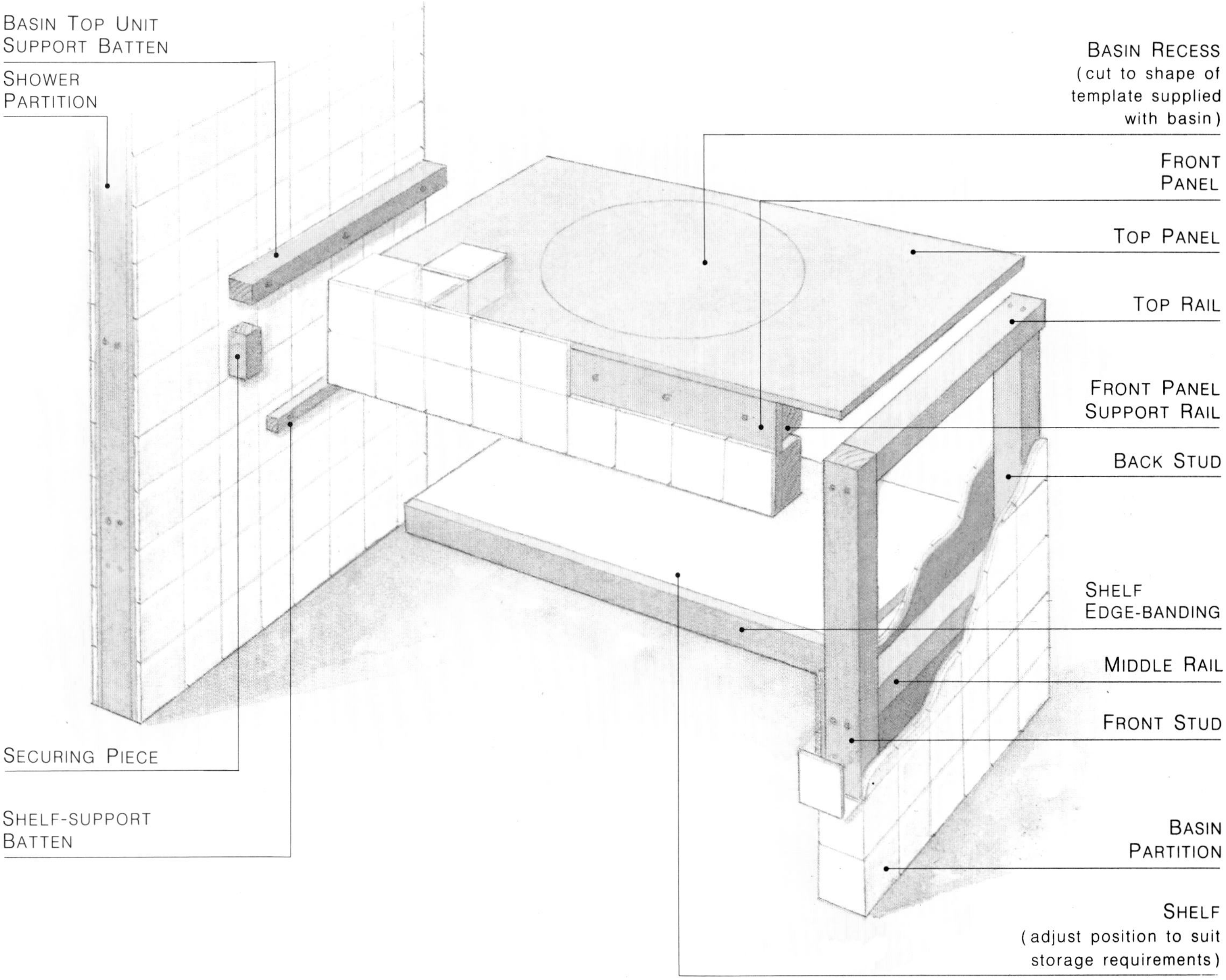
BASIN TOP UNIT SUPPORT BATTEN
SHOWER PARTITION
SECURING PIECE
SHELF-SUPPORT BATTEN
BASIN RECESS (cut to shape of template supplied with basin)
FRONT PANEL
TOP PANEL
TOP RAIL
FRONT PANEL SUPPORT RAIL
BACK STUD
SHELF EDGE-BANDING
MIDDLE RAIL
FRONT STUD
BASIN PARTITION
SHELF (adjust position to suit storage requirements)

TILED BATHROOM

FRONT PANEL

Measure the width of the recess from inside the basin partition to the side of the shower partition and cut a piece of ½in or ¾in (12mm or 19mm) water-resistant plywood to fit across this width. The depth of this piece should be enough to hide the underside of the basin. Work it out so that the total depth will coincide with whole tiles, after allowing for the thickness of the top panel.

TOP PANEL

Measure for the top panel to fit the width and depth of the alcove, and to finish flush with the front of the low partition. Cut the panel from ¾in (19mm) water-resistant plywood. Use a 2 x 3in (50 x 75mm) or a 2 x 2in (50 x 50mm) batten cut to the length of the front batten to join the top and front panels together at right angles. Make sure that the front panel rests under the top panel, and that there is a space at the end to slot over the end partition. Glue the batten in place and screw through the panels into it.

INSTALLING THE BASIN FRAME ASSEMBLY

To support the basin unit at the shower partition end, cut a 2 x 2in (50 x 50mm) batten to length and screw it to the side of the shower partition, screwing into the cross-rail inside the partition. It must be fitted exactly level with the top of the low partition. Rest the unit in place, but do not secure it yet as it will need to be removed for plumbing.

Cut the aperture for the inset basin by using the template supplied by the basin manufacturer. Use a power Saber saw to cut this hole, or do it by hand with a compass saw. Check that the basin fits in the hole, but do not install it until you have tiled the top panel.

Screw scrap pieces of 2 x 2in (50 x 50mm) lumber to the back of the front panel to secure it to the partitions at each side.

PLUMBING AND WIRING

At this stage the plumber can install the basin, shower tray, and bathtub, and the supply and waste pipes.

Inset showers can be installed now, and the pipework can be put in place for surface-mounted types, although the fixtures themselves are installed after tiling in both cases.

Also, have the wiring put in at this stage, with tails left protruding for lights, electric razor outlets, heaters, electrical showers, and so on to be installed later.

PERMANENT SECURING OF THE SIDES, BASIN, AND SHOWER UNITS

Attach all of the second sides to the partitions by nailing into the studs and rails. Screw the basin unit in place through the top panel into the partition and the support batten and through the scrap pieces to secure to the partitions at each side.

For the shower base, screw the front panel in place on to the front frame, and screw the top piece down on to the front and back frame. Insert silicone-rubber caulking between the frame and bathroom fixtures, where appropriate.

For the ceiling unit, screw the 2 x 2in (50 x 50mm) battens into

the plywood sides for the ceiling to fit correctly, and screw through the ceiling panel into the battens. However, if you prefer to do most of the tiling on a flat surface, do not secure the ceiling panel until it has been tiled, leaving off the tiles at the edges, at the points where you will be screwing through into the battens. Attach the ceiling panel in place, then tile over the screws.

TILING

Protect the bathroom fixtures while you are tiling, as they can be spoilt by adhesive and grout. If they are in wrappings, keep these on for as long as possible. Begin tiling *(see* **Techniques, page 94** *)*; below are some tips relevant to this project.

Tile the sides of the partition first, but note the middle rail positions before, so you know where to fit the shelf supports. Work from the front edge to the back so that any cut tiles will be at the back, against the wall.

Apply the shower ceiling tiles before securing the ceiling panel in place. Leave off the edging tiles so that you can screw the ceiling panel

---

1 **Assembly of Basin Top Unit from ¾in (19mm) Plywood**
Cut the top panel to the width and depth of the basin alcove. Glue and screw the top panel and front panel to a square batten so that they are at right angles, the front panel resting beneath the top panel.

2 **Making up the Under-basin Shelf Assembly**
Shelf is cut to inside width of recess and set back slightly from front of side partitions. Wooden edge-banding, glued and nailed to the front edge of the shelf, hides the shelf-support battens which are screwed to the partition units.

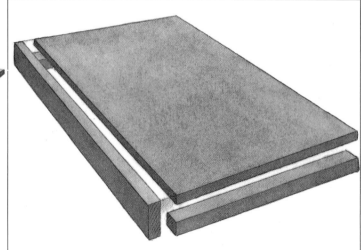

to its fixing battens. If you have already attached the ceiling panel, tile the partition walls up to it.

Tile the front surfaces next, that is, the front edges of the partitions, the front panels of the basin, shower tray, and bathtub panel.

Tile the top surfaces, that is, around the bathtub, basin, and shower. Around the bathtub, where a lot of water is likely to lie, put some extra thickness of adhesive around the outer sides of the tiles so they slope very slightly towards the tub.

Tile the walls and remaining partitions next. If you are fitting a glass shelf, apply tiles up to one tile's height below the level of the shelf on those walls where the shelf will be fitted. Fit the glass shelf (see below), then complete the tiling.

Finally, if you previously tiled the shower ceiling while it was flat, you can now attach the remaining tiles to the partition sides. These were initially left off in order to screw the ceiling unit to its fixing battens; they can be held in place with masking tape while the tile adhesive sets. If the shower ceiling has already been

installed, tile with the aid of a simple home-made lumber T-support. This is lightly wedged in place between the ceiling and the floor to hold each row of tiles in place while the adhesive sets. The support will be needed for about 15 minutes on each row.

After a minimum of 12 hours the joints between the tiles can be grouted with a waterproof grout, and the tiles can be polished clean.

Attach the bathtub panel, and any access panels, with dome-head screws. You can drill clearance holes with a masonry drill bit. Do not press too hard, and make sure that your electric drill is *not* switched to hammer action. Put a piece of masking tape on the tile where you want to drill the hole, to prevent the drill bit from skidding across the surface.

Finally, apply a silicone-rubber caulking to all joints between the bathroom fixtures and the ceramic tiles and to all internal corners where partitions meet the original walls. Caulks are available in white, clear, and a range of colors, and are supplied with full instructions. To eject a bead of the caulk, you usually

3 Securing a Glass Shelf Using Hidden Supports
The wall is chaneled to the thickness of the plaster for a batten which is attached at the back and sides of the alcoves. The shelf is made of tempered glass and rests neatly on the batten. After fitting, fill any gaps and finish tiling.

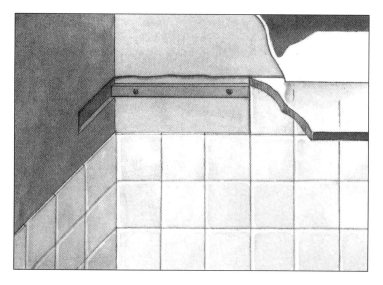

press a plunger with your thumb, although trigger-operated aerosol packs are also becoming popular.

GLASS SHELF

Setting a glass shelf in a wall is an unorthodox method of fitting, but, if properly done, the effect of having no visible means of support is well worth the effort. However, for an easier solution, rest the glass on rubber door stops screwed into the wall – two stops at each end – after the wall or partition has been tiled.

For a concealed attachment, ask your supplier what thickness of tempered glass you need for your span. Ours is $\frac{1}{2}$in (12mm) glass spanning 43in (1100mm). The glass must be cut to size and the edges polished.

Stop the tiles one tile's height below where you want the shelf. Cut a slot into the wall at the back and each end to the thickness of the plaster and about 1in (25mm) or so wide. Fix in place a thin batten to the thickness of the plaster, minus the thickness of the shelf.

Where the shelf meets the shower partition, you must cut a slot to the thickness of the glass in the facing panel. Do this either by drilling a row of overlapping holes with a diameter the same as the shelf's thickness, and chisel out the waste to make a straight-sided slot, or use a Saber saw or router to cut a neat slot.

Slot the shelf into place. This can be difficult and it may be necessary to cut away a little extra plaster above where the shelf has to go. Fill any gaps with wall filler or tile adhesive, then complete the tiling up to the shelf. Above the shelf you can add a mirror, or tile the wall.

UNDER-BASIN SHELF

This is made from $\frac{1}{2}$in (12mm) plastic laminate-faced particleboard, but you can use plywood if you are going to tile the shelf. Cut the shelf to the width of the recess and to

the required depth. It will look better if it is recessed back from the front edge a little way – $4\frac{1}{4}$in (108mm) (one tile's width) in our case.

Cut edge-banding from 1 × 2in (25 × 50mm) pine. Hold the shelf in a vise and glue and nail the edge-banding to the shelf's front edge so that the top edge of the edge-banding is flush with the shelf surface and the bottom edge hides the support battens. Punch the nail heads below the surface, fill holes, sand smooth, and apply a finish.

SHELF-SUPPORT BATTENS

These support the shelf at each side from behind the edge-banding to the back wall. Cut two pieces to length from 1 × 1in (25 × 25mm) lumber. Drill two clearance holes in each batten, then drill the sides at the marked levels. Countersink the holes and screw battens in place.

MIRROR

Attach the mirror to the wall with dome-head screws if it is drilled for these. If it is not, use corner fixing mirror plates. When using dome-head screws, put a tap washer over each screw behind the mirror to keep it slightly away from the wall. Whichever type of attachment you use, be careful not to over-tighten the fixing screws as you may crack the glass; ask your glass supplier for the correct screws and washers.

VALANCE

To conceal the overhead lighting, attach a valance above the mirror in the basin recess. Make it from $\frac{3}{4}$in (19mm) plywood cut to the width of the recess and to the depth of one tile. Cut two support blocks from 1 × 2in (25 × 50mm) lumber, about 1in (25mm) less than the valance depth, to fit behind the valance strip at each end. Screw these into the wall and the side partition in order to fit the valance in place.

PANELED BATHROOM

Often, the best ideas are the simple ones. Very few things in life are more unpleasant than trying to dry yourself with a damp towel, so if you install this room-width rod combined with a radiator you can remedy this forever. The rod here is made from chromed tube, but could be finished in colored enamel or be made in wood like the spar of a yacht.

All of the pipework in this bathroom has been hidden neatly behind a false wall which is simply constructed from painted tongued-and-grooved pine boarding. This is a particularly good solution, as a section of the paneling can be mounted on a batten frame to create an access panel which can be easily removed if you have any plumbing problems.

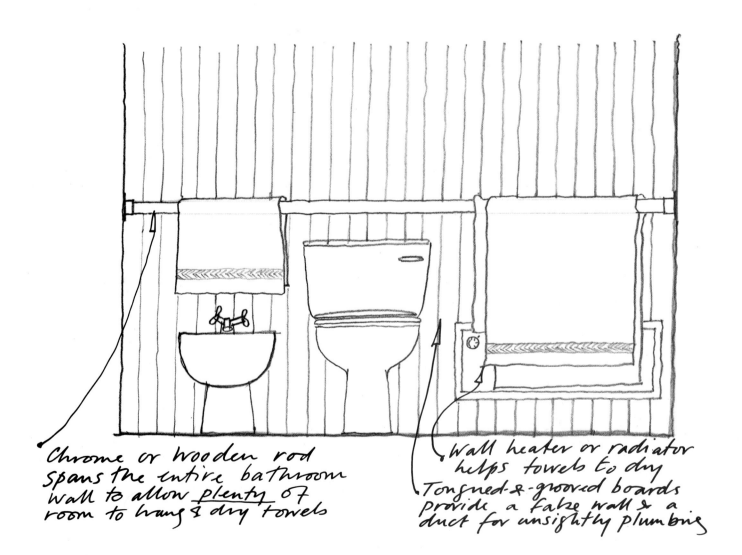

Chrome or wooden rod spans the entire bathroom wall to allow <u>plenty</u> of room to hang & dry towels

Wall heater or radiator helps towels to dry
Tongued-&-grooved boards provide a fake wall & a duct for unsightly plumbing

PANELED BATHROOM

Building a false wall is a clever way of concealing ugly pipework in the bathroom. The job is relatively easy if you are installing a new bathroom suite. However, if a suite is already installed, you may have to move one or more of the fixtures to make space for the new wall. Check that this is possible, bearing in mind the position of pipes and drains.

The false wall is made by attaching battens to the existing wall and covering them with lumber boards. These are normally tongued and grooved, and can range from plywood strips faced with an attractive veneer to solid lumber such as pine. Normally, they are attached vertically over horizontal battens.

The battens need only be of rough-sawn softwood, and should be at least 2 × 2in (50 × 50mm) if you intend to run pipes behind them. They should be fixed at centers of about 24in (610mm). There is no need to strip off any of the wall decoration before attaching the battens.

The spacing of the battens is determined largely by the thickness of the boards to be used, but also by the degree of rigidity required. It is important for the paneling to be more rigid in places where it may be leant against. As a guide, ⅜in (9mm) boards should have battens at centers of 16–20in (400–500mm), while ½in (12mm) boards need battens set 20–24in (500–610mm) apart.

Always begin and end battens a short distance from corners or ceilings so that nails do not have to be driven into the last few fractions of an inch (millimeters) of the boards, as this can cause splitting.

In order to bring all the battens flush with each other, plywood or hardboard shims may have to be used behind some of the screws. This will certainly be necessary with an undulating wall. Check the battens carefully with a long straight-edge, for unless they are completely flush, you will not be able to attach the boards to them properly.

The 2in (50mm) battens should provide enough space to conceal most bathroom pipes. If not, use thicker battens. Screw the battens to the wall, cutting out sections to accommodate pipework where necessary. However, if the wall is perfectly flat, you can secure the battens with masonry nails, provided they are long enough to go at least ½in (12mm) into the masonry.

Should you want to attach boards of random lengths for effect, then additional horizontal battens will be needed, spaced to suit your board lengths. Position boards so that the cut ends meet in the center of a batten and those at either end are both a similar width.

You can attach the boards with nails or with special clips which slot on to the tongue and are then nailed to the battens. Nailing through the face of the boards is the simplest and quickest method, but the nail heads must be punched below the surface and the holes filled with a matching wood filler. It is not necessary to match the wood exactly if the boards are to be painted.

MATERIALS

Part	Quantity	Material	Length
WALL BATTENS	As required	2 × 2in (50 × 50mm) (minimum) softwood	Width of wall
BOARDS	As required	⅜in or ½in (9mm or 12mm) thick boards	As required
TOWEL ROD	1	1½in (38mm) diameter aluminium, chrome, or wooden pole	As required
SUPPORT DISKS	2	¾in (19mm) MDF disks	As required

TOOLS

STEEL MEASURING TAPE

CARPENTER'S LEVEL

STRAIGHT-EDGE

SCREWDRIVER

NAILSET

HAMMER

SMALL HAND SAW

BACK SAW (fine toothed)

SABER SAW (or compass saw)

TONGUE-AND-GROOVE CLIPS

MITER BOX

POWER DRILL

SPADE BIT

COUNTERSINK BIT

MASONRY BIT

Nailing through the tongues with very thin brads provides an invisible attachment. These are driven at an angle into the tongue and are hidden by the groove of the next board. You may find that the wood splits in some cases, since dry pine is rather brittle. Do not worry if this should happen. Just break off any splinters; the splits will be covered by the groove of the next board, which is slotted over the tongue.

If the boards are to be nailed, attach the first with its groove in the corner, and check with a carpenter's level that it is standing plumb. Adjust the board as necessary before securing it in place by driving brads through the grooved edge. These are the only surface brads used and should be sunk below the surface of the board with a nailset. The holes should be filled with a matching wood filler.

1 Attaching Tongued, Grooved, and V-jointed Boards with Nails
First board, left, is scribed to side wall, ensuring board is vertical. Nail to batten, driving nail at an angle through grooved edge. Tap next board, right, over tongue and nail through tongue. Repeat for all succeeding boards.

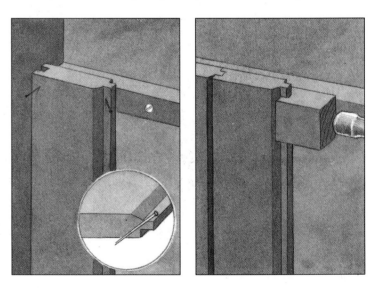

Nail the other side of the board, angling brads through the tongue. Fit a brad into each wall batten.

Tap the next board over the tongue to hide the brads. Protect the edge of the board from the hammer with a piece of scrap wood.

Clips are easy to use and provide a stronger attachment than brads, but are more expensive. They lock into the lower part of a groove.

The tongued edge of the first board goes into the corner you are starting from. Cut off the tongue with a fine-toothed back saw. Position the cut edge in the corner and nail it in place or use a special starter clip. Then secure the grooved edge with a clip. This is hidden by the next board inserted in the groove.

If boards of random length have to be butt-jointed at their ends, use a miter box with a right-angled slot for very accurate saw cuts. Do not fill the gaps between the joints.

The boards used in our bathroom were stopped short of the floor, giving an attractive finish. The lower edge was decorated with beading. To do this, attach a temporary

batten at the bottom at the required height above the floor, to serve as a finishing guide for the bottom edge of each board. When it is removed, the bottom edges of the boards will be flush with each other.

Glue and nail the beading in place along the lower edge of the boards. Also, fit the beading in the corners and along the ceiling line to hide gaps. It should be nailed to the walls or ceiling and not to the boards. Again, the heads of the brads should be sunk below the surface and the holes filled with a matching wood filler. If you prefer to avoid nail holes, fit the beading with an aliphatic resin glue.

It is advisable to provide easy access to pipework and joints for maintenance or repair. Therefore, attach a few strategic boards with screws rather than brads, cutting off the tongues, so that the boards in question can be lifted out easily. Make a feature of the screws by using dome-head or brass screws.

Although lumber boards provide an excellent way of covering up old or unsightly walls, they must never

be used on damp walls. The cause of the dampness should be traced and eliminated. The only form of dampness that they will cure is condensation, since the new wall surface will be warmer.

If an insulating blanket is to be applied between the battens to increase the heat retention of an outside wall, first cover the wall with vapor barrier (either polyethylene or building paper) and attach the battens over it. Although this will ensure that no dampness from the bathroom seeps through to the wall, it is not a cure for dampness or the structural damage that it can cause.

Finally, remember that all lumber can move with changes in moisture. Therefore, all boards should be conditioned before use by keeping them in the room in which they are to be used for about a week beforehand.

TOWEL ROD

A feature is made here of the towel rod, which runs the width of the bathroom. A $1\frac{1}{2}$in (38mm) diameter

anodized aluminium pole was chosen, although chrome or wood can be used instead. If the pole is very long, a couple of intermediate supports will prevent it sagging.

If you have to make your own support disks, use $\frac{3}{4}$in (19mm) MDF. To mark out a circle for a disk, draw around an object of a suitable size, such as a coffee mug. Cut the circle with a Saber saw or compass saw.

Mark off the circumference of the pole in the center of each disk and cut it out with a spade bit, or with a Saber saw or coping saw. Repeat for the other disk.

Countersink two holes in each disk, attach the disks to the pole, and get a helper to hold the pole level while you mark off the screw hole positions on the wall. Remove the pole and disks while the holes in the wall are drilled and anchored.

Replace the disks on the pole and get a helper to hold the pole while the screws are inserted. Use 2in (50mm) No 8 screws.

Fill the screw holes, sand down when dry, and apply a finish to the disks to match the pole or the wall.

② Using Clips
Saw off tongue. Push the board over a starter clip and secure grooved edge with clips.

③ Finishing the False Wall with Beading at the Bottom
Boards are attached to 2 × 2in (50 × 50mm) wall battens, or whatever thickness necessary to hide pipes. For neatness stop the boards short of the floor and nail a beading here.

④ Towel Rod Support Disks
Make support disks from $\frac{3}{4}$in (19mm) MDF and cut hole in center for rod using a Saber saw or a coping saw.

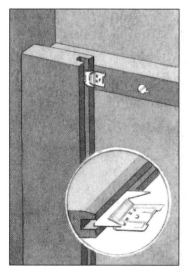

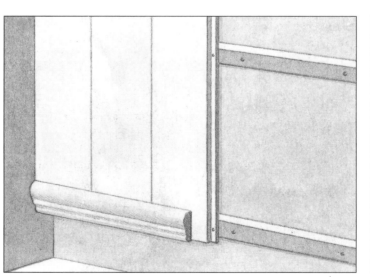

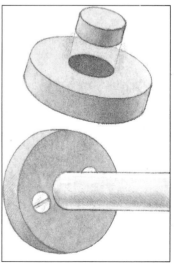

WARDROBE
WITH HINGED DOORS

I suppose the dream that most people want to realize when furnishing their bedroom is to be able to afford a complete and well-fitted wall of clothes storage units. Although very expensive to buy, these fitted units are relatively easy to build yourself.

Wardrobes never seem large enough to allow all your clothes to hang properly without being crushed, and there is always the problem of last season's clothes, which are not being worn but still have to be stored; bulky items such as bags and suitcases must also be considered. This simple but solid wardrobe has ample storage space for everything and will add value to your home should you wish to move in the future. Its simple wooden frame can be scribed to the wall, floor, and ceiling if they are uneven or sloping.

The main doors have framed panels, and the panels could be easily replaced with mirror if you prefer a reflective wall. The upper doors are hinged and fitted with a stay so they will remain open when you stow away your luggage.

The interior can be fitted with closet poles, shelves (either solid or slatted), and a shoe rail. A full-length mirror could be attached to the inside of one door.

A shoe rail is fitted into the bottom of the wardrobe

Wooden framework of wardrobe

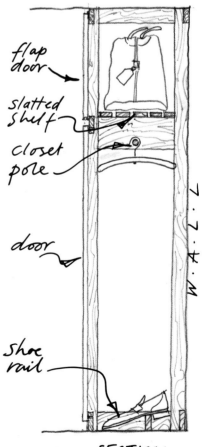

flap door

slatted shelf

closet pole

door

shoe rail

W·A·L·L

SECTION

door stay mechanism

top flap door lifts easily for storage of luggage and out-of-season clothes.

additional shelf above closet pole if required

Front elevation of wardrobe with masses & masses of space for clothes!

WARDROBE WITH HINGED DOORS

This wardrobe is comprised of three independent double-wardrobe sections linked together. Each section is designed as a free-standing unit to which you fit end panels if necessary. You can build as many sections as you wish, and the design allows for a single section to be built easily should your storage needs or available space require it. You can fit one or both end frames to the wall. In either case, an end panel is not needed to fit the frame at the end(s) adjoining the wall.

Buy the doors ready-made from a do-it-yourself store or lumberyard. The style is optional, but check that either a small version is available for the top cupboard, or that you can make smaller doors to match.

Alternatively, cut down a standard door to make small top ones.

To make the doors, laminated particleboard panels can be used, to which moldings can be nailed to give a paneled appearance. The size of the doors governs the overall dimensions of the framework. They should extend from floor to ceiling, with an equal allowance of just over 1in (25mm) at the top and bottom, and where the main doors and the top doors meet. The doors are recessed about $\frac{3}{8}$in (10mm) from the front edge of the frame for neatness.

The other important dimension is the inside depth of 24in (610mm), since this is the optimum for hanging and storing clothes.

TOOLS

STEEL MEASURING TAPE

ADHESIVE

CARPENTER'S LEVEL

HAND SAW

BACK SAW

DOWELING JIG

POWER DRILL (with twist drill bits)

ROUTER

CHISEL

MALLET

BAR CLAMP

SCREWDRIVER

TACK HAMMER and BRADS

ANCHORS (or cavity-wall fixings)

OPTIONAL TOOLS FOR SCRIBING

SABER SAW

COMPASS SAW

SURFORM or RASP

MATERIALS

Per *double* wardrobe section unless otherwise stated

Part	Quantity	Material	Length
DOORS			
2 large and 2 small to fit from floor to ceiling with an allowance of 1in (25mm) at top, middle, and bottom. Width of doors governs overall width of wardrobe			
FRAMES	(Quantities given are for one frame. Three frames required per double wardrobe)		
POSTS	2	2 × 4in (50 × 100mm) S4S softwood	Floor to ceiling height
CROSS RAILS	3	As above	16in (410mm), plus 2in (50mm) if using tenon joints
END PANELS	(Quantities given are for one end frame. Two end frames required per free-standing wardrobe)		
END PANELS, TOP AND BOTTOM	2	$\frac{1}{4}$in (6mm) laminated or plain plywood; width is distance between posts, plus 1in (25mm)	Height between top and middle rails, and middle and bottom rails, plus 1in (25mm)
BEADING		$\frac{1}{2}$ × $\frac{1}{2}$in (12 × 12mm) S4S softwood	Sufficient length to fit around perimeter of end panel
CLOSET POLE			
CLOSET POLES	2	1in (25mm) diameter dowel or broom handle	Distance between frames, plus 1$\frac{1}{2}$in (38mm)
SPACING RAILS			
SPACING RAILS	12	2 × 2in (50 × 50mm) S4S softwood	Width of door, plus $\frac{5}{32}$in (4mm), plus 1$\frac{1}{2}$in (38mm) if using tenon joints
SLATTED SHELF			
SHELF SLATS	7	1 × 2in (25 × 50mm) S4S softwood	Length of wardrobe, plus 1in (25mm)
TOP SHELF			
TOP SHELVES	2	$\frac{3}{4}$in (19mm) plywood; 22$\frac{3}{4}$in (580mm) wide	Distance between frames, plus $\frac{3}{4}$in (19mm)

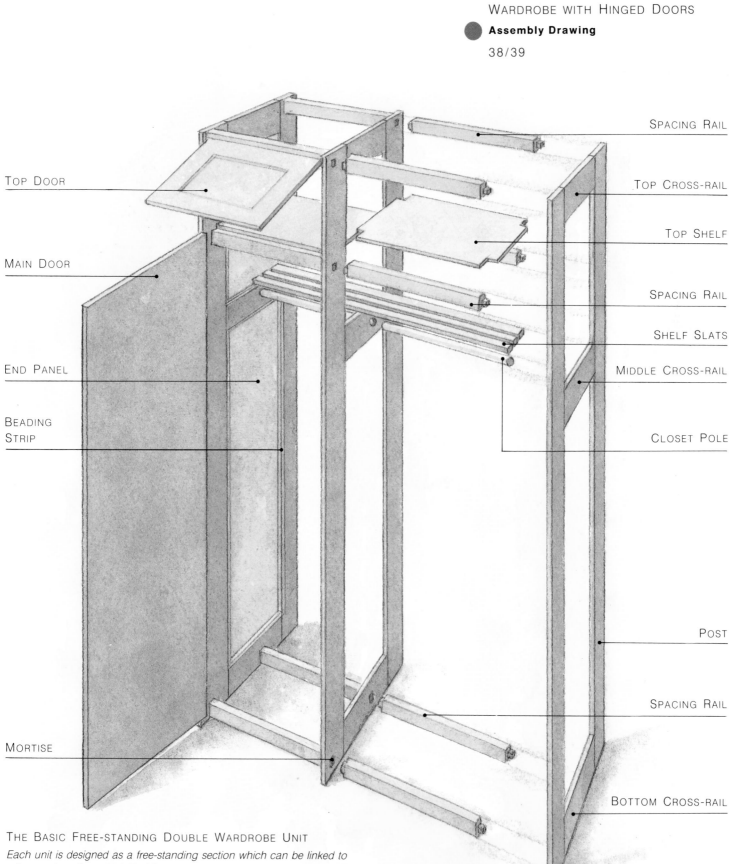

TOP DOOR

MAIN DOOR

END PANEL

BEADING
STRIP

MORTISE

SPACING RAIL

TOP CROSS-RAIL

TOP SHELF

SPACING RAIL

SHELF SLATS

MIDDLE CROSS-RAIL

CLOSET POLE

POST

SPACING RAIL

BOTTOM CROSS-RAIL

THE BASIC FREE-STANDING DOUBLE WARDROBE UNIT
*Each unit is designed as a free-standing section which can be linked to
other sections if required. End frame can be left open, or paneled-in.*

WARDROBE WITH HINGED DOORS

BASIC ASSEMBLY

FRAME ASSEMBLY

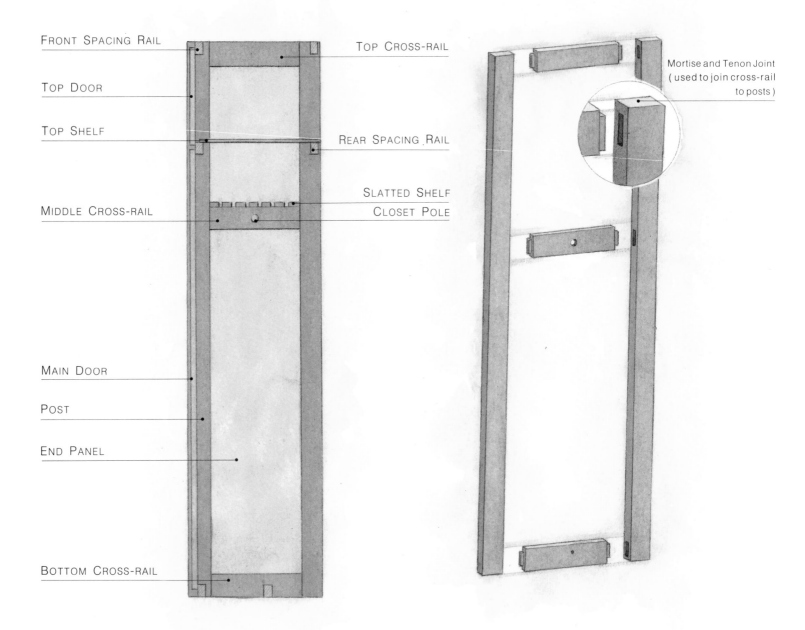

FRONT SPACING RAIL

TOP DOOR

TOP SHELF

MIDDLE CROSS-RAIL

MAIN DOOR

POST

END PANEL

BOTTOM CROSS-RAIL

TOP CROSS-RAIL

REAR SPACING RAIL

SLATTED SHELF
CLOSET POLE

Mortise and Tenon Joint
(used to join cross-rail
to posts)

1 **Components of the Wardrobe Shown in Cross-section**
The depth of the wardrobe is 24in (610mm) which is optimum for clothes
storage. Note that bottom rear spacing rail is set forward as shoe rack.

2 **Joining of the Cross-rails to the Posts**
Wardrobe frames are made by attaching three cross-rails between two posts
using glued mortise and tenon joints as shown, or dowel joints.

FRAMES

Measure for the height of the frames. If your floor or ceiling is uneven, make all the frames to the largest measurement and scribe them to fit.

To make the posts, cut two lengths of 2 × 4in (50 × 100mm) softwood to the required measurement. Side rails are fitted between the posts at the top, bottom, and at the height of the closet pole using glued mortise and tenon joints or dowel joints (*see* **Techniques, pages 88 and 90**). The tenons or dowels need only be about 1in (25mm) long.

Measure for the required length of the rails to fit between the posts (and add 2in [50mm] for the tenons, if you are using them) and cut three rails from the 2 × 4in (50 × 100mm) softwood. The top and bottom rails fit flush with the ends of the posts. The middle rail supports the closet pole bar.

In the center of the middle rail drill a 1in (25mm) diameter hole for the closet pole. This can be cut from 1in (25mm) dowel or a broom handle.

Decide how high you want the closet pole to be as this will determine the height at which you fit the middle rail. The height of the pole is governed by the configuration of the main doors and on the length of your longest item of clothing, when it is on a hanger.

Make up the required number of frames but do not drill the holes right through the end frames – these should be drilled to only half the thickness of the rail. Before drilling the holes, mark out their centers very accurately to ensure that the closet pole fits easily.

END PANELS

Measure for the two end panels. They should be cut to the height between the top and bottom rails and to the width between the posts, plus ½in (12mm) all around. Cut them from either veneer-faced particleboard or plywood, for a wood finish, or from plain plywood if you want a painted finish rather than a varnished effect.

Use a router to make a rabbet ½in (12mm) wide and ¾in (19mm) deep

❸ Attaching Spacing Rails to Wardrobe Frame
Mortise and tenon joints are used to join the spacing rails to the wardrobe frames. Each tenon is half the thickness of the lumber that is used for making the posts and the cross-rails.

❹ Attaching the End Panels
End panels are secured in rabbets cut inside the frames and held with beading (below).

FRAME AND END PANEL
Detail inside the wardrobe (above) shows spacing rail shoe rack and frame scribed around baseboard.

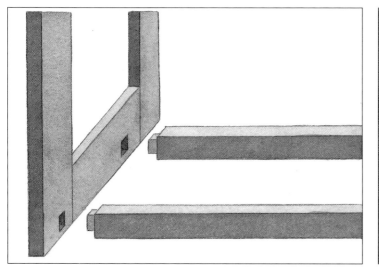

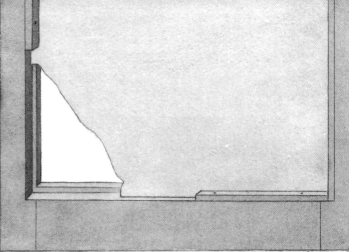

WARDROBE WITH HINGED DOORS

around the inside of the frame. Do not fit the panels yet as you will need to fit a bar clamp through the frames when assembling them later. Repeat the process to fit the other end panel if your chosen design calls for a second one.

SPACING RAILS

The 2 × 2in (50 × 50mm) rails fit between each frame at the top, the bottom, and between the two rows of doors. They are also fitted using either mortise and tenon or dowel joints (see **Techniques, pages 88 and 90**). Each tenon should be half the thickness of a post so that one tenon each side will meet the other in the middle of a post.

Cut each spacing rail to the width of the door, plus $\frac{1}{8}$in (4mm) for clearance all around the door, plus the depth of the tenons if you are using them. Cut the required number of spacing rails to length, allowing for six between each frame.

The three front rails are set back from the front face of the posts by the thickness of the doors plus $\frac{3}{8}$in (10mm). The bottom back rail is set

forward about 9in (225mm) from the back edge to act as a shoe rail. The top and middle back rails are set forward about $\frac{1}{2}$in (12mm) to allow for easy scribing of the frame to the wall.

CLOSET POLES

Cut the required number of closet poles to the same length as the spacing rails, including an allowance for tenons so that they will meet in the middle of the posts, as with the spacing rails. If you plan to secure the rails with dowels, you must still remember to allow extra length on these poles, so that they meet in the middle of the posts.

INSTALLING THE FRAMES

Position one frame at a time and scribe it to fit at the wall, floor, and ceiling (see **Techniques, page 91**). Ensure that each frame is level with the next.

Scribe around the baseboard or remove it and replace it later. Mark where each frame will sit and identify each so that its position will not be interchanged. Fit the first end frame

WARDROBE INTERIOR
Generous storage space is provided by a slatted shelf (above) and a sturdy wooden hanging bar.

1 **Assembly of Slatted Shelf**
Slats form shelf on middle cross-rails. Cross-rails are drilled to take the closet poles.

2 **Top Door Hinging and Handle Detail**
Top doors hinge on a door lift mechanism which is screwed to the tops of the side frames. Note the rabbet on the bottom of the door edge to create a finger-hold for easy access.

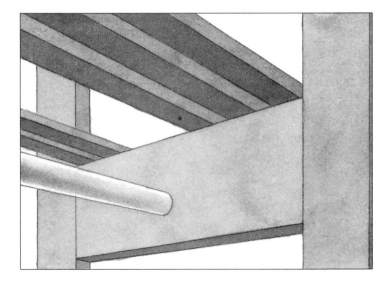

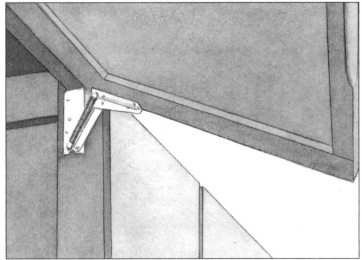

in place using corner brackets at the ceiling and floor on the inside *(see* **Techniques, page 85** *)*. Ensure that the frame is plumb. If you are fitting it to the wall at the end, allow a 1in (25mm) gap. This will be covered later with a scribing fillet. Otherwise, screw into the wall, placing a 1in (25mm) spacing batten between frame and wall.

ATTACHING THE SPACING RAILS

Glue and fit the spacing rails and the closet pole in position into the first end frame. Position the next frame with the joints already glued. Secure the two frames with bar clamps across the width and allow time for the glue to set. Repeat this operation for as many frames as you are using, fitting each frame as you go.

ATTACHING END PANELS

Fit each end panel into the rabbet in each end frame. To secure the panel, use beading nailed on the inside to finish flush with the frame.

SLATTED SHELF

The slats run the whole length of the wardrobe, resting across the middle rails of the frames. The outer ones butt against the posts and the others are spaced equally between them. If you have to join lengths, butt-join them at a frame. Nail the slats down to each rail.

TOP SHELF

Each $\frac{3}{8}$in (10m) plywood top shelf rests on the middle spacing rails. It is set back a little from the front edge to conceal it, or, better still, rabbeted into the rail. Cut each shelf to meet its neighbor in the middle of the center post. Cut out notches in the corners to fit around the posts. Nail down the shelf to the spacing rails at the back and front. Repeat for each shelf.

MAIN DOORS

Hang the main doors using 3in (75mm) brass butt hinges *(see* **Techniques, page 92** *)*. Fit the hinges so the doors are set back $\frac{3}{8}$in (10mm) from the front edge. This will mean that you must not pull your doors open by more than 90° or the hinges will be weakened or pulled out. If you feel it necessary (if children will use them, for example), attach stops to ensure this will not happen.

Finally, fit handles of your choice and any form of paneling or applied decoration to the front of the doors.

TOP DOORS

These are hinged at the top. It is well worth buying a special hinge called a "door lift mechanism" which acts as a combined hinge and stop *(see* **Techniques, page 93** *)*. A spring action allows the door to be raised and remain in an open position.

Rout out a rabbet or bevel to create a handle along the bottom edge of each door. Fit magnetic catches to all the doors (see **Techniques, page 93** *)*.

SCRIBING FILLET

If you are attaching the frame to a wall at one or both ends, use a scribing fillet to fill the gap between the wall and the end frame; this will ensure a neat and secure fit. Set the fillet back from the frame the same amount as the doors. It can then be painted to match either the doors or the wall.

BASEBOARD

If there is a baseboard already in position against the wall, it will be necesary to remove the baseboard from between the frames. Cut a piece of baseboard to length so that it fits exactly the space between each frame.

③ Hinging of Main Door
Brass butts are used to hinge main doors which are set back from edge of frames.

WARDROBE STORAGE SPACE
With doors open, the wardrobe gives access to solid top shelf, slatted shelf, and closet pole.

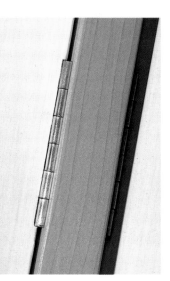

FOLDING SCREEN

Screens have many uses in the home, subdividing space both physically and visually, and defining different areas.

This screen has a second use as a clothes horse for a bedroom or hall. With the addition of a hanging rail, wooden knobs, and a shelf, it can quickly become an elegant and simple wardrobe for use in a spare room, for a weekend guest, or in a student's or child's bedroom.

The geometric grid of wooden slats can be rearranged to make the particular pattern of your choice. The slats can either be painted, stained in a variety of colors, or left simply as natural wood. Alternatively, each panel of the screen can be covered on one side with a light fabric to provide a more private room divider. The traditional and ingenious webbing hinge allows the panels of the screen to fold flat when not in use.

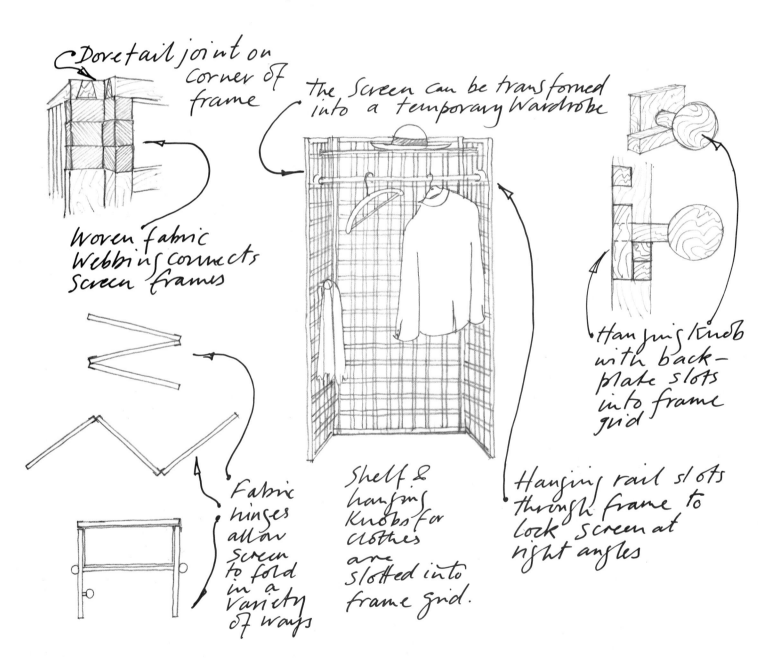

Dovetail joint on corner of frame

Woven fabric webbing connects screen frames

the screen can be transformed into a temporary wardrobe

Fabric hinges allow screen to fold in a variety of ways

Shelf & hanging knobs for clothes are slotted into frame grid.

Hanging knob with back-plate slots into frame grid

Hanging rail slots through frame to lock screen at right angles

FOLDING SCREEN

You can use a folding screen to divide space in a room or to hide ugly corners and unsightly features in various rooms in the home. If you nail lightweight gauze to one side of an open frame, it will provide a screening effect without reducing light transmission too much. Alternatively, you can nail or staple an opaque material to one side to form a solid screen. For our screen, we created a trellis.

TOOLS

STEEL MEASURING TAPE

TRY SQUARE

UTILITY KNIFE

MARKING GAUGE (or mortise gauge)

SLIDING BEVEL

DOVETAIL SAW or FINE-TOOTH BACK SAW

COPING SAW

HAND SAW, POWER CIRCULAR SAW, or POWER SABER SAW

PARING CHISEL $\frac{1}{2}$in (12mm)

DOWELING JIG

DRILL (hand or power)

CENTERPOINT BIT

SPADE BIT (or auger bit if hand brace is used)

MALLET (or hammer and scrap of wood for driving in dowels)

BAR CLAMPS (or band clamp or folding wedges)

TACK HAMMER (or similar lightweight hammer)

FINISHING SANDER or HAND SANDING BLOCK

STAPLE GUN (or tack hammer and tacks)

PAINTBRUSH 1$\frac{1}{2}$in (38mm)

MATERIALS

Note: Quantities are for one frame; three frames required

Part	Quantity	Material	Length
OUTER FRAME UPRIGHTS	2	1 × 2in (25 × 50mm) S4S softwood	5ft 8in (1730mm)
OUTER FRAME TOP AND BOTTOM RAILS	2	1 × 2in (25 × 50mm) S4S softwood	28in (710mm)
HORIZONTAL FRAME CROSS BATTENS	15	1 × 1in (25 × 25mm) S4S softwood	Approximately 26in (660mm)
VERTICAL FRAME CROSS BATTENS	6	1 × 1in (25 × 25mm) S4S softwood	Approximately 5ft 6in (1680mm)
BATTEN FIXING DOWELS	42	$\frac{1}{4}$in (6mm) dowel	1$\frac{3}{16}$in (30mm)
HANGING RAILS	As required	1in (25mm) dowel	Distance between screen frames, plus approximately 1$\frac{1}{2}$in (38mm)
HANGING RAIL ENDS	6 (2 per rail)	3in (75mm) or 2$\frac{1}{2}$in (63mm) diameter wooden ball	
SHELF	1	$\frac{1}{2}$in (12mm) plywood, about 12in (300mm) deep	Approximately 30in (760mm)
KNOB BACK PLATE	1	1in (25mm) S4S softwood, about 3in (75mm) wide	Approximately 5in (125mm)
KNOB STOPPER BATTEN	1	1 × 1in (25 × 25mm) S4S softwood	Approximately 5in (125mm)
KNOB DOWEL	1	1in (25mm) dowel	3in (75mm)
KNOB END	1	2in (50mm) diameter wooden ball	

Using traditional fabric hinges which fold in both directions allows the screen to be used in either a Z-shape, or in a U-shape so that rails can be hung across its width for a temporary wardrobe. Additionally, a detachable shelf can be added. It fits neatly above the hanging rail. Also, wooden knobs can be slotted into the screen wherever required for hanging clothes. When not in use, the screen can be simply folded flat for easy storage.

The screen can be made from as many panels as you require. Ours comprises three, each 5ft 8in (1730mm) high by 28in (710mm) wide. The cross battens within the outer frame create spaces 3in (75mm) square. Each frame is made with dovetail joints at the corners for strength. However, you may prefer to use dowel joints (see **Techniques, page 90**) at the corners. These are perfectly reliable if glued securely with an aliphatic resin glue.

MAKING THE SCREEN PANELS

The outer frame of each panel is cut from 1 × 2in (25 × 50mm) S4S (smooth 4 sides) lumber and is assembled flat. For each panel, two uprights and two rails (top and bottom) are required. Our uprights are 5ft 8in (1730mm) long and the rails are 28in (710mm) long.

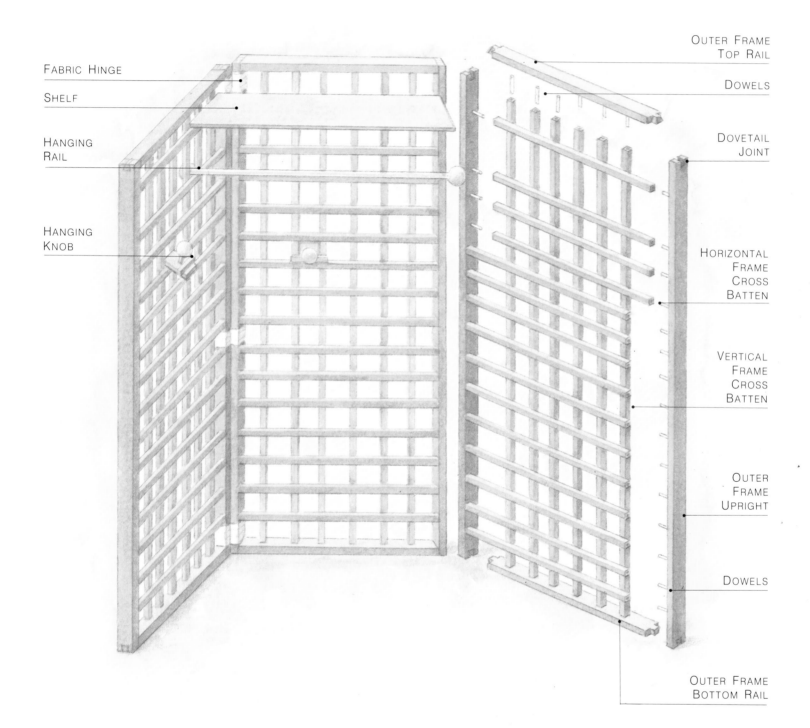

FABRIC HINGE

SHELF

HANGING
RAIL

HANGING
KNOB

OUTER FRAME
TOP RAIL

DOWELS

DOVETAIL
JOINT

HORIZONTAL
FRAME
CROSS
BATTEN

VERTICAL
FRAME
CROSS
BATTEN

OUTER
FRAME
UPRIGHT

DOWELS

OUTER FRAME
BOTTOM RAIL

FOLDING SCREEN

DOVETAILING THE TOP AND BOTTOM RAILS

A full description of how to make a basic dovetail joint is given elsewhere in the book (see **Techniques, page 89**); included here are instructions specific to this project. Set your marking gauge to the thickness of the rail and mark off this distance from the end of the short rail, continuing the line around both faces and edges. Repeat for each end of the top and bottom rails.

Mark off the approximate pin shape on to the end of a piece of scrap wood of the same stock size, and work out the correct setting for your marking or mortise gauge.

Using the gauge, mark off the lines of the top of the pin on to the outer face of the rail. Then, using the sliding bevel, mark out the pin on to the ends of the rails using a pencil sharpened to a chisel point. Continue the lines of the bottom of the pin around on to the inner face, using a try square (fig 1). Repeat the procedure for each end of the top and bottom rails of each frame.

Hold the rail upright in a vise and saw down through each pencil line to the depth of your marked line, using a dovetail saw or a fine back saw. Then hold the rail horizontally in the vise to remove the shoulders of the tail, to leave only the "pin" (center part), sawing down to the marked line of the tail. Repeat for each end of the top and bottom rails.

DOVETAILING UPRIGHTS

Using the marking gauge as before, set it to the stock thickness and mark off the ends as before, continuing the lines right around the rail. Number each joint to ease assembly later.

Lay a short rail lengthwise on top of a long one to mark off the thickness of the pin. Then stand the short rail upright at the end of the long one to mark the cut-out to house the pin on to the long rail, which will be the "post" (fig 2).

Repeat for each joint, making sure that you number them as you go, as they will not be interchangeable. Extend the marks on to the ends with a try square. Mark each end of the uprights in this way.

To make the vertical cuts, the post must be held firm. It is best to place it upright in a vise, supported with long shim pieces clamped on either side, and then to stand on steps to reach it. Cutting *inside* the pencil lines (the waste side), make angled cuts to the marked line.

To remove the waste from the post, use a coping saw to cut down the center and out to each side, being sure to stay a little way inside the marked lines. Pare down to the sides with a paring chisel. Repeat for the other ends of the uprights and fit the joints together, matching the identification numbers. Identify the faces of the rails and uprights as well as their pins and tails. It is a good idea to do a practice joint first on a piece of scrap wood.

CROSS BATTENS

With the frame dry assembled, measure the internal dimensions and cut the cross battens from 1 × 1in (25 × 25mm) S4S to these measurements. In our case, there are 15 horizontals and 6 verticals per panel. Dismantle the frame.

We used ¼in (6mm) diameter hardwood dowels, 1¼in (30mm) long to attach the cross battens to the outer frame. (This is about the right size. If your dowel sizes are different, you will have to adjust the dimensions accordingly.)

Using a doweling jig, drill the ends of all the battens in their centers to a depth of about ¾in (19mm), using a ¼in (6mm) diameter centerpoint or brad-point drill bit (also called a lip-and-spur drill bit).

MARKING DOWEL HOLES

Take the vertical battens and bunch them up together on the top and bottom rails, against the shoulders of the dovetail joints. Measure to the other shoulder and divide this figure by the number of spaces. This will give you the gap between all the battens. Measure this distance in from the shoulder, plus half the thickness of the batten. The first dowel hole center will be on this line. From then on, mark the dowel hole center lines according to the spacing measurements already calculated. The final distance should be

---

1 Dovetailing the Rails
Depth marked all around; top of pin marked. Dovetail marked on end; bottom of pin marked.

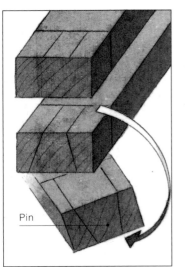

2 Marking the Frame Uprights
Depth and thickness of rail pin marked; then shape of pin marked on frame upright.

3 Completing the Outer Frame Dovetail Joints
Top rail pin is cut with a fine back saw or dovetail saw. Frame upright post is cut with dovetail and coping saws. Clean up the joint with a paring chisel for a good, secure fit.

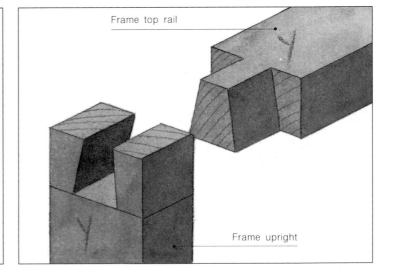

Top rail

Frame upright

Frame top rail

Frame upright

the same as the first. Transfer the hole marks to all the other top and bottom rails.

To mark the dowel hole positions widthways, find the center of the rail width and measure out from it exactly half the thickness of the vertical batten. (This will be nearer $\frac{3}{4}$in [19mm] than the nominal 1in [25mm].) Draw a line down the rail. Where it crosses the dowel hole lines will be the dowel hole center points.

Repeat the above procedure for the horizontal battens on the upright posts, spacing them apart by the same distance as you did for the vertical battens. Space one of the battens down from the top, and then the rest of them up from the bottom. This will create a larger gap between the top horizontal batten and the next one down, which is where the removable shelf fits.

To mark the dowel hole positions widthways, measure exactly half the batten thickness out from the center, but in the opposite direction to that of the vertical battens. This ensures that the horizontal battens are fitted *exactly* in front of the verticals.

Drill all the marked holes to a diameter of $\frac{1}{4}$in (6mm) and a depth of $\frac{1}{2}$in (12mm).

ASSEMBLING THE PANELS

To assemble a panel, put a small amount of glue in each dowel hole in the top and bottom rails. Insert the dowels. Put a small amount of glue into the hole on each end of the vertical battens and push them into all the dowels.

Take one of the posts and glue and assemble both of the dovetail joints on one side. Then glue and dowel all of the horizontal battens into the upright post. Glue and join the second post, the dovetails, and the dowels simultaneously.

Use bar clamps (or a band clamp or folding wedges) across the panel to pull the joints together. Then, using a spacing batten, check that all the spaces are equal, and nail the battens to each other where they cross, using the spacing batten as you go. Repeat the procedure for the other two panels and paint, stain, or varnish to finish according to your decorative scheme.

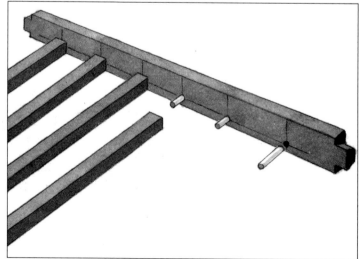

④ Working Out Dowel Hole Spacings for Vertical Battens
Bunch the vertical battens together on top and bottom rails against shoulders of the dovetail joints. Measure gap to other shoulder and calculate spacing of battens.

⑤ Vertical Batten Assembly
Mark and drill dowel holes in rails. Apply glue and insert dowels. Glue holes in battens and attach dowels.

TEMPORARY WARDROBE
The screen can be easily converted to a wardrobe for hanging clothes. Useful when guests come to visit.

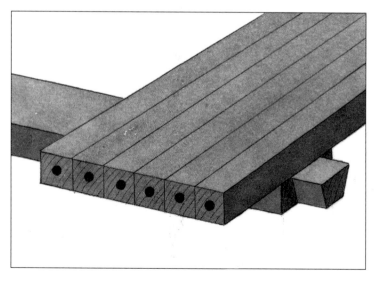

FOLDING SCREEN

FABRIC HINGES

The three panels are joined together with fabric hinges at the top, bottom and middle. Each hinge comprises three separate strips of 1in (25mm) wide webbing the color of which matches the finish of your screen.

The two outer strips are identical and are attached first, leaving a space for the middle one, which is fitted the opposite way around. The outer strips are about 12in (300mm) long, and the middle one about 11¼in (280mm). Cut the webbing overlength, try it in place, and cut off the excess. Follow fig 3 to attach the first strip, by stapling or tacking it on to one panel and joining it to the next by winding round in a figure eight to cover the ends. Put temporary staples in to hold the webbing firm while winding it around. Staple the last face to the panel and push the end through on to the next face to conceal the staples on both panels. Repeat for the other outer strip.

Follow fig 3 to fit the middle strip. You will not be able to take this one around as far as the others, concealing only the first set of staples. Push the end through on to the next face as before. Make three hinges each between adjacent panels.

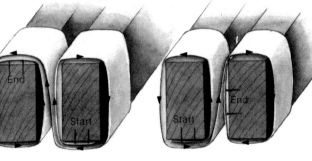

outer strips   middle strip

DETAIL OF SCREEN HINGE
The fabric hinge (above) enables the screen to fold in two directions. Fabric matches screen color.

1 Assembling Horizontals
Apply glue and push first upright post into dovetails of top and bottom rails. Glue and dowel.

2 Assembling the Second Upright Post on the Assembly
Glue and join dovetails and dowels at same time. Batten left out at top.

3 Making the Hinges
Wind webbing fabric around the panel uprights in the direction of the arrows to form a secure hinge.

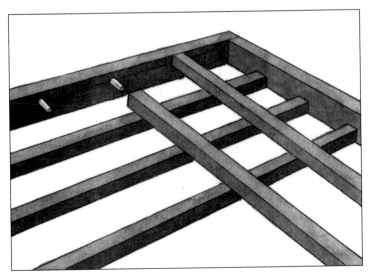

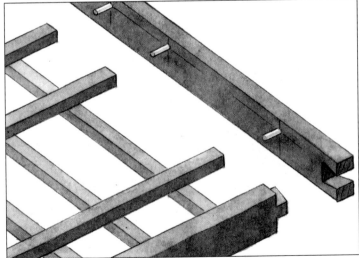

HANGING RAILS

Set the screen up in a U-shape and measure across for the hanging rails from the outside edges of the cross battens, plus $\frac{3}{4}$in (19mm) at each end to go into 3in or $2\frac{1}{2}$in (75mm or 63mm) diameter wooden knobs. Cut the required number of rails from 1in (25mm) dowel. Each rail will be about 30in (760mm) long if made to our dimensions.

Put each knob in turn into a vise and drill into it to a depth of $\frac{3}{4}$in (19mm) using a 1in (25mm) spade bit. Assemble the rails by gluing the dowel and knobs together and slot them into place where desired.

SHELF

Use $\frac{1}{2}$in (12mm) plywood to make a shelf, if required. This rests on top of the cross battens and is easily removable when you want to fold the screen. Cut the shelf to fit (about 12in [300mm] deep). As it is intended as a temporary shelf it should not be used to store heavy items, although it is perfectly adequate for lightweight clothing.

HANGING KNOBS

To make a back plate, use a piece of 1in (25mm) S4S softwood as high as one section of the outer dimensions of the horizontal battens and of a width to fit easily between the vertical battens.

Using a 1×1in (25×25mm) offcut, cut a piece as long as the outer dimensions of one upright batten to the next. This is the stopper. Put the back plate into position in one square and the stopper in place to the front of it, to mark where it will fit on the back plate.

Drill a 1in (25mm) diameter hole in the back plate, its center about 1in (25mm) up from the top of the stopper position, to a depth of $\frac{1}{2}$in (12mm). Cut a piece of 1in (25mm) dowel to a length of 3in (75mm) and glue it in the hole. Glue and nail the stopper in place on the back plate.

Drill a 1in (25mm) diameter hole to a depth of $\frac{3}{4}$in (19mm) into a 2in (50mm) diameter wooden knob and glue it in place on top of the dowel. Hanging knobs can be slotted into any square.

④ Nailing the Battens
Clamp frame, and, with an offcut to check the exact dimension of the spacings, nail battens together.

⑤ Making the Hanging Rail and Hanging Knobs
Hanging rail is 1in (25mm) diameter dowel with wooden knobs at ends. Hanging knobs comprise batten across back plate on which wooden knob on short dowel is attached.

DETAIL OF WARDROBE
As a wardrobe, the screen is a stylish addition to any bedroom or spare room.

JAPANESE WARDROBE

Although this particular sliding screen has been designed as a wardrobe in a bedroom, the same construction would look equally stylish in a living room. To me, there is nothing more serene than a traditional Japanese room and I have tried to echo this serenity in this project.

The frame that holds the screens must form a rectangle, with every corner an exact right angle. For this reason you will notice that there is a scribing fillet around the edge of the screen's frame to take up the inevitable inaccuracies of your floor, walls, and ceiling.

The screens are simply constructed to a rectangular module which will vary according to the exact size of the wall you wish to screen. I have used a tough, natural, creamy cotton rather than traditional Japanese paper to back the screen, but you could alter the material to suit your own decorative scheme.

One of the great bonuses of this screen wall, apart from its storage potential, is that a light inside the wardrobe will be gently diffused by the fabric, to provide an elegant, soothing background to your bedroom or living space.

PLAN OF WALL FIXING

Block to take up unevenness between wall, ceiling & frame

WALL anchor

sliding door track

sliding Door

cloth backing held in place by fillet

scribing fillet painted the same colour as Wall and Ceiling

SIDE ELEVATION OF CEILING FIXING

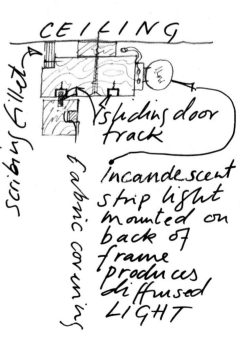

CEILING

scribing fillet

fabric covering

sliding door track

incandescent strip light mounted on back of frame produces diffused LIGHT

FRONT ELEVATION OF JAPANESE WARDROBE.

Gap between wall and wardrobe frame filled with scribing fillet.

PLAN

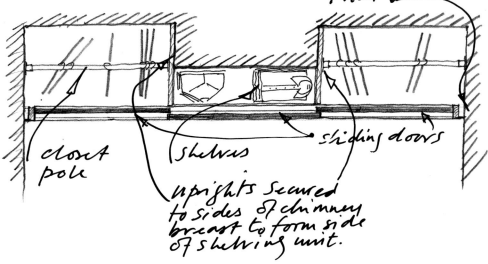

closet pole

shelves

sliding doors

uprights secured to sides of chimney breast to form side of shelving unit.

JAPANESE WARDROBE

The lightweight sliding doors of this fitted wardrobe are divided with a narrow trellis-like framework and backed with fabric to produce a Japanese-style "wall". The doors are designed to fit wall-to-wall across a room with (or without) a chimney breast and alcoves. Lights are installed behind the doors to light the inside of the wardrobe and to throw a diffused light into the room when the doors are closed – an excellent way to create a restful atmosphere in a bedroom, for example.

In our design, the doors slide in front of the chimney breast, completely hiding it. Vertical partition panels are fitted to each side of the chimney breast, protruding a short distance in front of it and allowing narrow shelves to the width of the chimney breast to be incorporated.

If you are building this wardrobe on a flat wall, you will still need to include two internal partition panels to support the closet poles and the deep shelves. However, in this case all the shelves will be deep, and three closet poles can be attached instead of two.

For neatness, where there is no chimney breast, make the vertical partition panels as two narrow, plywood-covered box sections.

MATERIALS

Part	Quantity	Material	Length
PARTITIONS	2	$\frac{3}{4}$in (19mm) plywood, lumber core or particleboard. Width as inside depth of cupboard; 21in (530mm) in our case	Room height
DEEP SHELVES	4	As above; $20\frac{1}{2}$in (518mm) wide to allow for thickness of edge-banding	Distance between partition panels and side walls
SHALLOW SHELVES	6	$\frac{3}{4}$in (19mm) plywood, lumber core or particleboard. Width as distance from chimney breast to front of partition panels, less $\frac{1}{2}$in (12mm)	Distance between partition panels
SHELF EDGE-BANDING	10	$\frac{1}{2} \times 1\frac{1}{2}$in (12 × 38mm) S4S pine or hardwood	As shelf lengths
DEEP SHELF REAR SUPPORT BATTENS	4	1 × 1in (25 × 25mm) S4S softwood	As shelf length
DEEP SHELF SIDE SUPPORT BATTENS	8	1 × 1in (25 × 25mm) S4S softwood	Shelf depth, less $1\frac{1}{2}$in (38mm)
SHALLOW SHELF REAR SUPPORT BATTENS	6	1 × 1in (25 × 25mm) S4S softwood	As shelf length
SHALLOW SHELF SIDE SUPPORT BATTENS	12	1 × 1in (25 × 25mm) S4S softwood	Shelf depth, less $1\frac{1}{2}$in (38mm)
CLOSET POLES	2	Chrome pole or 1in (25mm) diameter dowel	Alcove width
RAIL SUPPORT BATTENS	4	1 × 3in (25 × 75mm) S4S softwood	2 at 21in (530mm) 2 at 24in (610mm)

DOOR FRAMES

Part	Quantity	Material	Length
TOP AND BOTTOM RAILS	2	2 × 4in (50 × 100mm) S4S softwood	Room width, plus 6in (150mm)*
UPRIGHTS	2	As above	Room height*
TOP SCRIBING FILLET	1	1 × 1$\frac{1}{4}$in (25 × 32mm) S4S softwood	Room width*
SIDE SCRIBING FILLET	2	As above	Room height*

DOORS (quantities are for one door. Our project uses three doors)

Part	Quantity	Material	Length
STILES (side rails)	2	2 × 2in (50 × 50mm) S4S softwood	Internal height of door frame, less clearance for door hardwear
TOP RAIL	1	2 × 2in (50 × 50mm) S4S softwood	One-third of internal width of frame
BOTTOM RAIL	1	2 × 4in (50 × 100mm) S4S softwood	As above
HORIZONTAL TRANSOMS (central bars)	3	1 × 1in (25 × 25mm) S4S softwood	Internal width of door frame, plus 1in (25mm)
VERTICAL MULLIONS (central bars)	2	1 × 1in (25 × 25mm) S4S softwood	Internal height of door frame, plus 1in (25mm)
SIDE FABRIC FASTENING BATTENS	2	$\frac{3}{8} \times \frac{3}{8}$in (9 × 9mm) S4S softwood	Internal height of door frame, plus 4in (100mm)
TOP AND BOTTOM FABRIC FASTENING BATTENS	2	$\frac{3}{8} \times \frac{3}{8}$in (9 × 9mm) S4S softwood	Internal width of door frame, plus 4in (100mm)

*Dimensions are oversize to allow for trimming later.

COMPONENTS OF THE MAIN ASSEMBLY

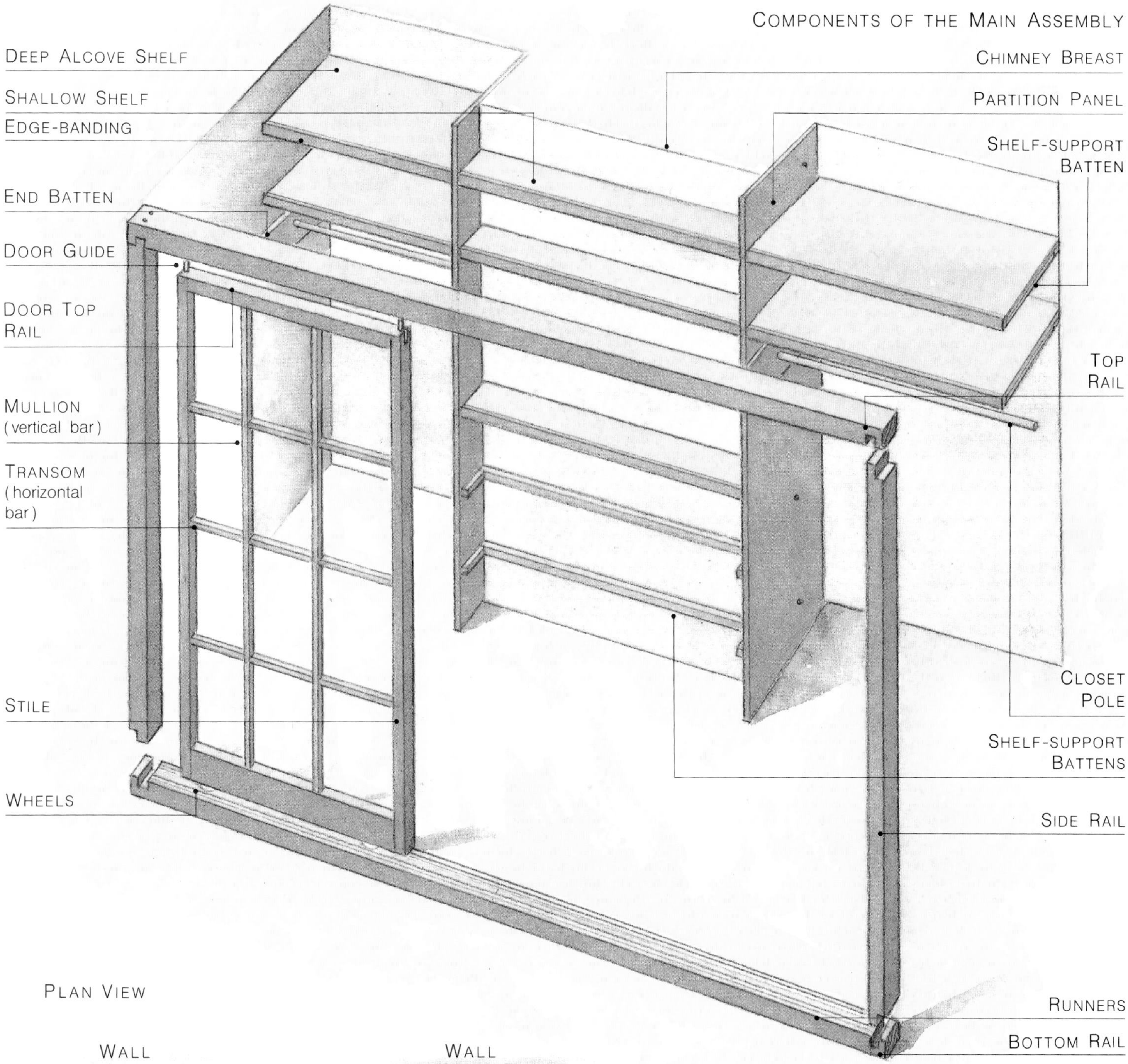

CHIMNEY BREAST

PARTITION PANEL

SHELF-SUPPORT BATTEN

DEEP ALCOVE SHELF

SHALLOW SHELF

EDGE-BANDING

END BATTEN

DOOR GUIDE

DOOR TOP RAIL

MULLION (vertical bar)

TRANSOM (horizontal bar)

TOP RAIL

STILE

WHEELS

CLOSET POLE

SHELF-SUPPORT BATTENS

SIDE RAIL

RUNNERS

BOTTOM RAIL

PLAN VIEW

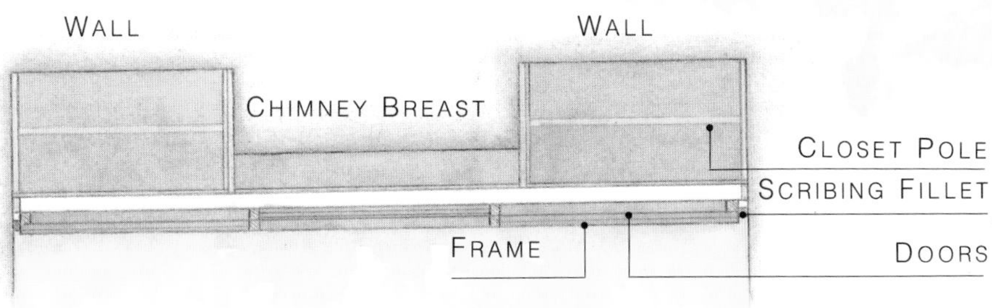

WALL   WALL

CHIMNEY BREAST

CLOSET POLE

SCRIBING FILLET

FRAME   DOORS

Japanese Wardrobe

Layout

Decide on the internal layout of the wardrobe: the height of the closet poles, the position of the shelves, etc. Our shelves are spaced at 14in (350mm) centers down the chimney breast, with closet poles in the alcoves at either side and two deep shelves above the main closet pole.

Mark the internal depth of the wardrobe (ours is 24in [610mm], which is a good width for hanging clothes). Mark all the way around: on walls, floor, and ceiling. Start by marking a point 24in (610mm) out from the rear wall at each end and mark on to the side walls just above the level of the baseboard. Hang a chalked plumb line on each wall to align with these marks and snap the line to mark a vertical line on each wall. Snap a chalked line on to the ceiling to join these two lines. Finally, repeat for the floor. This line will be the inside of the door frame.

If you are working in an old house where the room is not square, you may not be able to measure out from the end wall to fix the position of the door frame. Instead, you may have to use the 3-4-5 method (see **Techniques, page 80**) to get the frame at right angles to one, or both, of the side walls. Mark the frame position on the floor, then snap vertical lines on the side walls and finally snap a line on the ceiling. Also, in an old house the floor, walls, and ceiling may slope a lot. If so, you may have to use shims under the floor rail and scribe wide shims between the sides and top of the door frame to fill odd-shaped gaps. It is vital that the door frame is square, regardless of how much the walls, floor, and ceiling are out of true.

After marking the inside of the door frame line, measure back 3in (75mm) and snap another line around the walls, floors, and ceiling parallel with the first line. This inside line marks the front edge of the shelves and partition panels.

Partitions

Cut partition panels to the height of the room from $\frac{3}{4}$in (19mm) plywood, lumber core, or particleboard. These are fitted to each side of the chimney breast. Their width is the distance from the rear wall to the inside line (21in [530mm] in our case).

Position the panels, check that they are plumb (shim them if necessary), and screw and anchor them to each side of the chimney breast.

If there is no chimney breast, make and install two partition panels as follows: each partition is made from two panels of $\frac{3}{8}$in (9mm) plywood on a 1 × 2in (25 × 50mm) S4S lumber framework. The panels should extend from floor to ceiling, and should be slotted over 1 × 2in (25 × 50mm) battens which are screwed to the rear wall, floor, and ceiling to give a strong, invisible support. Within the panels, position cross battens to provide extra support at levels which coincide with the shelf and closet pole positions when these are installed.

Shelves

On the back and side walls mark the positions of the undersides of the shelves, using a pencil, carpenter's level, and straight-edge (or a planed length of lumber batten).

Cut shelf-support battens from planed pine to run along the back and side walls, allowing for the thickness of the edge-banding on the front of the shelves. The battens are 1 × 1in (25 × 25mm) (see **Materials list, page 56**).

Drill and screw the battens to the rear walls, side walls, and partition panels, ensuring that they are level with one another, and level on each side of the partition panels. Anchors will be required where the battens are attached to masonry walls.

Use a filler to cover the screwheads. Paint the battens.

Cut the shelves to fit from $\frac{3}{4}$in (19mm) plywood, lumber core, or particleboard. Nail $\frac{1}{2}$ × 1$\frac{1}{2}$in (12 × 38mm) edge-banding to the front edge of each shelf, flush with the top edge of each shelf. The edge-banding will overhang to hide the support battens.

Closet Poles

Use proprietary chrome rails and end supports, or 1in (25mm) diameter wooden dowels, cut to fit the widths of the alcoves. The dowels are fitted to 1 × 3in (25 × 75mm) end battens cut to fit the width of the cupboard from the frame to the back wall in the case of the end battens, and from the front edge of the partition panels to the back wall for the inside battens. To form the closet pole, the inside battens are drilled centrally to hold the dowels and the end battens drilled to match. To fit the pole, screw the end batten to the wall, slot the inside batten on to the dowel, then put the dowel in the attached batten, and finally screw the other batten in place, checking with a carpenter's level that the pole is level. Make sure that the poles on each side are level with one another, at the desired height.

Sliding Door Frame

The frame is built to give a 1$\frac{1}{4}$in (30mm) gap at the top of the frame and at each side, to allow for scribing for a neat finish while coping with baseboard and irregularities in the wall and ceiling surfaces. When you measure, allow for these spaces and make the frame to these external dimensions.

The frame is made from 2 × 4in (50 × 100mm) S4S (smooth 4 sides) lumber and is constructed with dado joints (to be precise, rabbet-and-dado joints) at the corners. This type of joint is very strong, but the short grain on the outside of the grooves is a weakness and therefore the top and bottom rails are left about 6in (150mm) overlength to form "horns" which are sawn off after the joint is made.

Put the top and bottom rails side by side and clamp them together. Mark the external width of the frame on to them. Rest a frame upright across the top and bottom rails to mark off the internal dimensions and then mark this line square on the top and bottom rails using a try square and a utility knife. Set a marking gauge to half the thickness of the uprights and mark off from the internal face, squaring across as you go with a try square and a utility knife (*see* **Techniques, page 80**).

Use a router to cut out the dado (or groove) as marked, or saw along the inside (waste side) of the dado lines using a fine-toothed back saw and then chisel out the waste wood.

Cut the frame uprights to length. (Note that these fit into the bottom of the dados.) Using the marking gauge as set for marking out the dados, mark off for the rabbets at the ends of the rails which will fit into the dados.

Cut out the waste with a back saw so that the rabbets fit securely in the dados.

Dry assemble the frame to check that the external dimensions are accurate enough to fit the room size with approximately 1¼in (30mm) spaces at the top and at each side of the frame. These will be filled by the scribing fillets, which will ensure a neat fit.

Take the frame apart and install the sliding door hardware. The method of fitting depends on the type and you must follow the manufacturer's instructions. It is very important to choose door hardware in which the wheels run along a bottom track, rather than hang from a top rack, otherwise our frame will not be suitable. It is much easier to fit this bottom-running track and the guide track at the top before the frame is finally assembled.

Assemble the frame, gluing the joints and screwing through the top and bottom rails into the uprights. At this point the frame must be braced square before the glue sets. Do this by nailing two diagonal braces on opposing corners following the 3-4-5 method of bracing (*see* **Techniques, page 80**).

INSTALLING THE FRAME

Lift the frame into position, ensuring that the upright rails are centralized between the side walls, with a 1¼in (30mm) gap at each side. Use a carpenter's level to check that the bottom rail is absolutely level, and if necessary adjust it with shims. With the diagonal braces still in position, screw the bottom rail to the floor after scanning the floor with a metal detector to ensure that the screws will not puncture pipes or wiring just beneath the floorboards. Use 3in (75mm) No 10 woodscrews, and, if possible, try to coincide the screws with the positions of the floor joists (floorboard fixing nails will indicate their location).

Check that the frame is vertical, then drill the side rails and wall at about 24in (610mm) intervals so that the frame-fixing screws complete with anchors already threaded part of the way can be inserted through the frame and into the wall. Before tightening the screws, insert shims between the uprights and the wall at the attachment points, keep-

ing the shims 1in (25mm) back from the front edge of the frame so that the scribing fillets can later be fitted between the frame and the wall. Check that the frame is still square by measuring across the diagonals, to ensure that they are of an equal length. If necessary, adjust the shims on either side.

Drill and screw the top rail to the ceiling, using 4in (100mm) No 12 screws, and screwing into the ceiling joists where possible. As with the uprights, at the screw positions, insert shims between the top of the rail and the ceiling before finally tightening the screws.

Check again that the frame is square, and then remove the bracing battens.

Between each side and the walls, and between the top rail and the ceiling, scribe a fillet made from ¼in (6mm) plywood to the wall and to the ceiling to fill the space. Attach the fillet by screwing into the shims.

Fill over the screwheads and, when dry, paint the frame the same color as the wall so that it blends with the rest of the room.

❶ Shelf Construction and Attachment of Shelf-support Battens
Shelves have edge-banding on front edges to hide the support battens and to stiffen the shelves to help prevent them from sagging. Remember to allow for the thickness of the edge-banding by setting back the side battens.

❷ Shelf Edge-banding
Plywood, lumber core, or particleboard shelves have hardwood edge-banding on front edge.

❸ Rabbet-and-Dado Joints
Rabbet-and-dado joints are used at the corners of the frame. Note the horns which are cut off later.

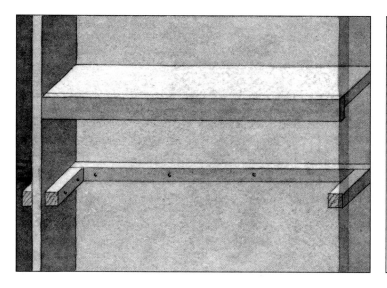

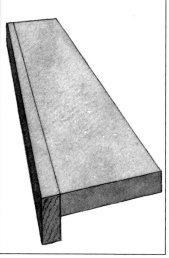

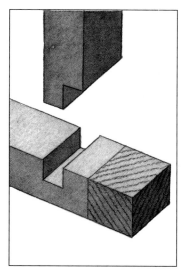

Japanese Wardrobe

Sliding Doors

Work out the external dimensions of the doors. For the door height, measure the height of the internal frame, allowing for the clearance specified in the instructions supplied with the sliding door hardware. For the width, divide the internal width of the frame by the number of doors required (we use three), allowing for doors to overlap each other by the thickness of the door stiles.

Using lumber as specified in the Materials list (page 56), cut the door stiles (vertical side members) slightly overlength and mark on them the positions of the top and bottom rails. Haunched mortise and tenon joints are used to joint the door components at the corners (*see* **Techniques, page 89**).

Cut the top and bottom rails to length and chop out the mortises in the stiles, then cut the tenons on the rails. The stiles are left overlength at this stage to avoid breaking out the end of the mortise while cutting it.

Dry assemble the door frame and check that the joints fit well.

Repeat the procedure for the other doors.

To make the transoms (horizontal internal bars) on each door, measure the internal width between the stiles, and cut three transoms to this length, plus 1in (25mm). (The number of transoms can be varied according to the size of the doors you are making.) Measure the distance between the top and bottom rails and cut two mullions (vertical bars) to this length, plus 1in (25mm). (Again, the number can be varied to suit the door size.) The bars are joined to the frame with bare-faced mortise and tenon joints, and where they overlap they are joined with cross-lap joints.

Take the frame apart and cut the mortises for the sliding door wheels in the bottom edge of the bottom rail (see the manufacturer's instructions).

Work out the spacing for all the internal bars and mark them on the inside faces of the frame. Set the mortise gauge to the full thickness of the 1 x 1in (25 x 25mm) bars, and gauge a line from the back of the door frame to mark the front positions of the bars.

Using a square-edge chisel (a mortise chisel is ideal, although an ordinary firmer chisel will do), or a router cutter, chop out, or rout, mortise slots to ½in (12mm) depth, and to half the thickness of the square bars by their full width.

Set the marking gauge to the width of the chisel or router cutter that you have used for cutting the

mortises, and using this setting, mark off the thickness of the tenons on the ends of the internal bars. Re-set the gauge to ½in (12mm) and mark off the lengths of the tenons on both ends of each bar. Cut the (bare-faced) tenons. When fitted, the back of each bar should lie flush with the back of the door frame.

Cut cross-lap joints at the intersections of all of the bars (*see* **Techniques, page 86**).

Start assembly by gluing the cross-lap joints and assembling the bars carefully, as they are easy to break. Assemble the top and bottom rails into the mullions, gluing all the joints beforehand.

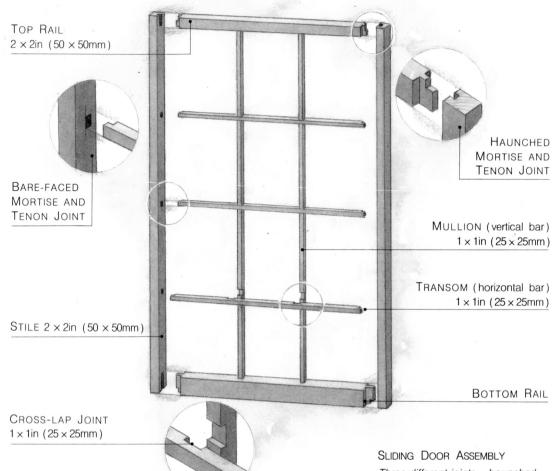

TOP RAIL
2 × 2in (50 × 50mm)

HAUNCHED
MORTISE AND
TENON JOINT

BARE-FACED
MORTISE AND
TENON JOINT

MULLION (vertical bar)
1 × 1in (25 × 25mm)

TRANSOM (horizontal bar)
1 × 1in (25 × 25mm)

STILE 2 × 2in (50 × 50mm)

BOTTOM RAIL

CROSS-LAP JOINT
1 × 1in (25 × 25mm)

Sliding Door Assembly

Three different joints – haunched tenon, bare-faced tenon, and cross-lap – are used in assembly.

Apply glue to the mortises and shoulders on one side of the doors and assemble the stile on this side of the tenons of the top and bottom rails and transoms simultaneously.

Repeat the procedure to attach the second stile.

Put bar clamps across the doors in line with the transoms, or put a band clamp right around the door. Check that the door is flat and square (the diagonals should be equal).

When the glue has set, remove the clamps and cut the excess lumber off the door stiles. Use a sharp plane to skim the faces of the doors to ensure that all the joints are flush.

JAPANESE WARDROBE

With the lights switched on, this wardrobe becomes an interesting trellis-like framework. The diffused light behind the fabric panels creates a restful backdrop in any room.

Repeat for the other doors. If you find these joints too hard to make, or too time-consuming, the door could be doweled together *(see* **Techniques, page 90** *).* Dowel joints are perfectly secure when glued with an aliphatic resin glue.

To fit the fabric behind the door, a groove is formed in the back of the door frame, and the fabric is laid in the groove, where it is then held in place with a batten pressed into the groove. Use a router to make the groove, which should be ⅜in (9mm) wide and the same depth. The groove is cut in the back of the door frame, its outer edge 1in (25mm) from the inside of the frame.

Cut a ⅜in (9mm) square batten and check that it is a tight fit when slid into the groove. If necessary, plane it to fit. Cut lengths of batten to fit the groove, mitering the corners.

Following the door hardware manufacturer's instructions, fit the wheel into the mortises previously cut in the bottom of the doors, and fit the guides to the tops of the doors.

Try the doors in place and check that they run correctly. If necessary, adjust the door hardware according to the manufacturer's instructions. Paint or finish the doors as required.

For the fabric we used 50% polyester/50% cotton sheets. Cut and fit the fabric by laying the door

① Attaching the Fabric Behind the Door Using Battens
To fit the fabric neatly, it is held in a groove in the back of the door by a batten which fits into the groove, holding the fabric taut. Miter the corners of the battens for a neat effect.

frame down and draping the fabric over it. You will need a helper to keep the fabric taut. Fit one long edge, screwing the batten in place to hold the fabric down. Pull the fabric taut to fit the opposite edge in the same way. Fit one end like this, and finally fit the opposite end in the same way. Screw the battens in place rather than nail them, as this allows the fabric to be removed and cleaned.

Fit the doors in place *(see* **Techniques, page 92** *).*

Wire in the internal lights at the back of the door frame. However, check the relevant codes to ensure that wiring regulations are compatible for use in enclosed wardrobes.

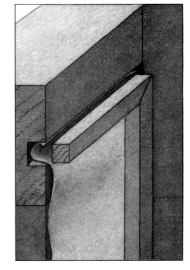

BED WITH TRUNDLE DRAWER

A lack of adequate storage space for blankets and unseasonal clothing is a perennial problem in bedrooms.

This generous bed provides storage space under the mattress, in a pull-out trundle drawer, and beneath the head-board, which is padded to make sitting up in bed and reading a book a real pleasure. The bed is designed so that it is easy to dismantle should you wish to move house, something that is quite often a problem with conventional double and king-size beds.

The loose covers of the headboard and footboard are easily removable for cleaning and can be made from fabric to coordinate with the other soft furnishings in your bedroom.

Generous storage space at the head and in the foot of the bed

pull-on loose covers fit over 1" (25mm) foam glued to the foot & head-boards

Velcro fastening

Angled back provides comfortable support for reading in bed.

pull-out drawer on castors slides underneath foot of bed.

SIDE ELEVATION OF BED

Mattress

slatted mattress support rests on sides of bed.

storage.

Storage drawer on castors

cross rails.

pivot for head board

Head board pivots forwards.

EXPLODED ISOMETRIC

pullout drawer with footboard loose covered in fabric

cross rails must be firmly fixed as they are fundamental to the solidity of the bed.

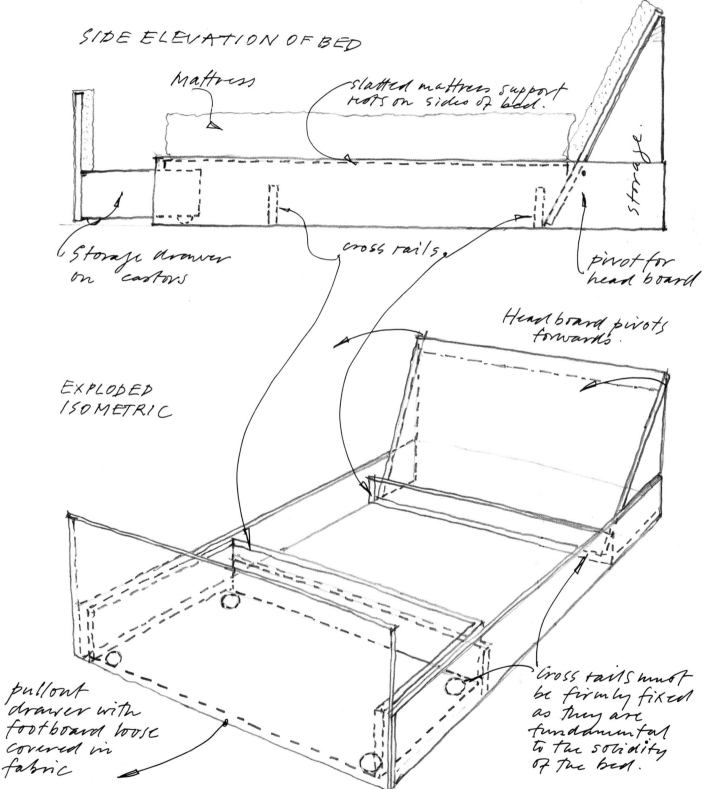

BED WITH TRUNDLE DRAWER

The bed should be assembled in the room for which it is intended. However, it can be taken apart and reassembled if necessary – when moving to a new house, for example.

Firstly, decide how large the bed is to be. The length will be determined by that of a standard mattress – 6ft 6in (2m) – plus 14in (350mm) for the headboard section. When the bed is positioned in the room, there must be sufficient space between its end and a wall or furniture for the trundle drawer to be pulled out by means of the footboard. The drawer shown is 24in (610mm) long.

The width of the bed is again determined by the size of the mattress. The "king size" mattress here is 6ft (1.8m) wide, but the bed can be made for one of 5ft (1.5m) or 4ft 6in (1.35m). It can also be adapted for a single-width mattress. The bed's height is also optional. Ours is 18in (450mm), offering plenty of storage space below.

The angled headboard provides comfortable support when you are sitting up in bed, and the upholstered top panel is readily removable to give access to ample storage space in the headboard section.

Further long-term storage space – for duvets and other bedding, for example – is available below the bed. This is reached by removing the mattress and the central slatted section of the mattress support.

The main components of the bed are constructed from ¾in (19mm) plywood, MDF (medium-density fiberboard), or particleboard. The edges of the latter will need an edge-banding of hardwood molding, which must be allowed for when calculating the dimensions. The Shaker-style pegboard shown in the photograph on page 64 is simple to construct. It consists of a lumber batten attached around the room at picture-rail height which is attached with hanging pegs at regular intervals. The pegs are used for storage, to hang curtains or pictures.

MATERIALS

Part	Quantity	Material	Length
THE BASE			
SIDE PANELS	2	¾in (19mm) MDF or particleboard	Length of mattress plus 14in (350mm) × required height
CROSS DIVIDERS	2	As above	Width of mattress × height of sides less 4in (100mm)
CORNER BATTENS	4	2 × 2in (50 × 50mm) S4S softwood	Height of cross dividers
HEADBOARD			
TRIANGULAR HEADBOARD SUPPORTS	2	¾in (19mm) plywood, MDF, or particleboard	23 × 45in (575 × 1125mm), divided diagonally into two pieces
TRIANGULAR FILLERS	2	As above	As required to fit
CROSS RAIL	1	1 × 3in (25 × 75mm) S4S softwood	Width of mattress
HEADBOARD SECTIONS	2	¾in (19mm) plywood, MDF, or particleboard	Width of mattress (see text for height)
STRENGTHENING BATTEN	1	2 × 2in (50 × 50mm) S4S softwood	Width of mattress less 1½in (38mm)
MATTRESS SUPPORT SECTION			
SIDE RAILS	2	2 × 3in (50 × 75mm) S4S softwood	Length of mattress, plus approximately 3in (75mm)
END RAIL	1	As above	Width of mattress
CENTER RAIL	1	As above	Length of mattress, plus approximately 3in (75mm)
SLATS	As required	1 × 3in (25 × 75mm) S4S softwood	Width of mattress
CROSS BATTENS	4	1 × 3in (25 × 75mm) S4S softwood	Internal distance between cross dividers
TRUNDLE DRAWER			
FOOTBOARD	1	½in (12mm) MDF	Width of bed less ½in (12mm) × height as required
DRAWER SIDES	2	As above	Height of sides of bed less 6in (150mm)
BACK	1	As above	Height of drawer sides × width of mattress less 2in (50mm)
BASE	1	As above	Internal dimensions of trundle drawer

BED ASSEMBLY AND MAIN
COMPONENTS

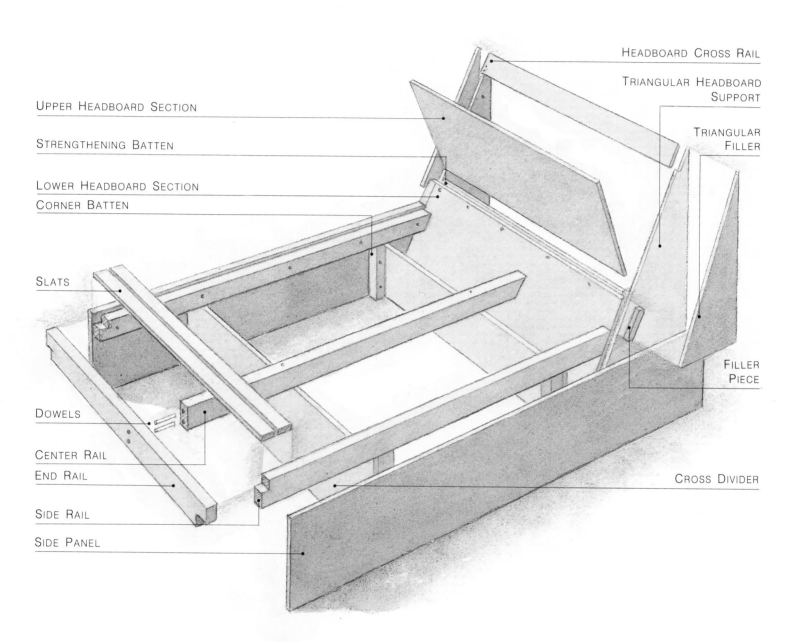

UPPER HEADBOARD SECTION

STRENGTHENING BATTEN

LOWER HEADBOARD SECTION
CORNER BATTEN

SLATS

DOWELS

CENTER RAIL
END RAIL

SIDE RAIL

SIDE PANEL

HEADBOARD CROSS RAIL

TRIANGULAR HEADBOARD
SUPPORT

TRIANGULAR
FILLER

FILLER
PIECE

CROSS DIVIDER

THE BASIC CONSTRUCTION OF THE BED
*All the main components of the bed are shown
here, except for the cross battens which fit under
the slats, and the trundle drawer which fits
under the bed end.*

BED WITH TRUNDLE DRAWER

TOOLS

STEEL MEASURING TAPE

TRY SQUARE

SPACING BATTEN

HAND SAW

POWER DRILL

BACK SAW

ROUTER

SCREWDRIVER

CLAMPS

HAMMER

PUTTY KNIFE

PLANE (or sanding block and sanding paper)

THE BASE

Cut two side panels from $\frac{3}{4}$in (19mm) plywood, MDF, or particleboard to the mattress length plus 14in (350mm) × required height. This one is 7ft 8in × 18in (2.35m × 450mm).

You will also need two cross dividers and four corner battens. Measure 24in (610mm) in from each end of the side panels and mark the positions of the cross dividers. Drill and countersink the corner battens on one face. Check that they are square with a try square. Then glue and screw them to the sides, inside the positions for the cross dividers and flush with the bottom edge.

Put the cross dividers in position against one of the sides, flush with the bottom edge (and outside the four corner battens), then drill, countersink, and screw through the dividers into the corner battens (fig 1). Do not reinforce this fixing by gluing, since it can then easily be taken apart should the need arise.

Put the other side panel in place and fit in the same way.

HEADBOARD

By dividing diagonally, cut two triangular headboard supports from one rectangle measuring 45 × 23in (1125 × 575mm).

HEADBOARD CROSS RAIL

This supports the headboard at the top. Cut one length from 1 × 3in (25 × 75mm) lumber, to the width of the mattress.

MAKING THE FRAME

Lay down one of the triangles and stand the cross rail on end, flush with the front edge of the triangle at the top, and as far to the point as it will go without overhanging the back. Mark its outline on to the end of the triangle. Repeat on the other triangle (fig 2).

Using a back saw or a Saber saw, cut inside the marked lines to remove the waste. This will then create a notch for the headboard cross rail to sit on.

Fit the two triangular supports inside the sides, at the head end, flush with the ends of the sides. Drill and countersink the inside of the triangles in at least four places each side, and screw one to each of the side panels (fig 3).

Put the cross rail in place. Drill and countersink the cross rail and screw it into the triangle's notches, keeping the screws low in the cross rail. Make sure that the ends of the cross rails are flush with the outside of the triangles (fig 4).

For the triangular fillers (fig 5), position a piece of MDF on the side panel. Line it up with the back edge of the triangular support and mark the triangle on to it. Cut out this triangle and repeat for the other side. Fit the fillers in place by drilling, countersinking, and screwing from the inside of the triangular supports. Use three screws on each side.

The headboard consists of two pieces, one above the other, cut to the width of the mattress. For the height of the lower piece, measure up the triangular support from the floor to about three-quarters of the

1 Attaching the Cross Dividers to the Side Panels
Glue and screw the corner battens to the side panels, then position the cross dividers against the battens, flush with the bottom edge, and screw in place through the dividers and into the battens.

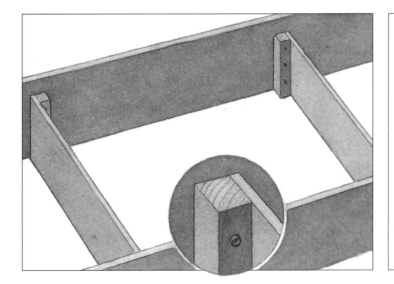

2 Headboard Cross Rail
Hold the cross rail on end at the top of the triangular support and mark out the notch.

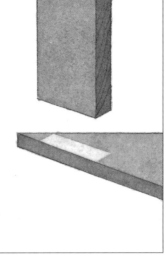

3 Attaching the Triangular Headboard Support
Headboard supports are screwed to the insides of side panels.

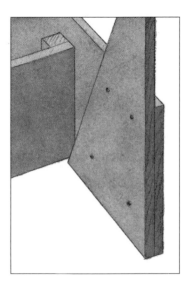

way up the thickness of the mattress, with the mattress in place. The higher piece measures the distance from that point to the top of the triangle plus $\frac{1}{2}$in (12mm). The extra portion serves as a fingergrip for access to the storage below.

STRENGTHENING BATTEN

The strengthening batten is cut from 2 × 2in (50 × 50mm) softwood to the width of the mattress minus the thickness of the two triangular supports (1½in [38mm]). Glue and screw the lower headboard section to the front edges of the triangular supports. Put the strengthening batten at the top of the lower headboard section on the underside, and clamp it in place half-way up its thickness, thereby creating a $\frac{3}{4}$in (19mm) rabbet for the top part of the headboard to locate in. Drill, countersink, and screw through the lower headboard section into the batten. Try the top headboard piece in place, then remove it for covering. The upholstery will bring it flush with the sides of the triangular fillers for a tidy finish.

Hold a piece of 1 × 1in (25 × 25mm) softwood batten against the gap between the top of the lower headboard section and the side panel. Mark off the top and bottom and cut with a back saw. The bottom will be at an angle to fit the side of the bed. Glue and nail or screw the batten in place to each side (fig 1, page 70). Plane, then sand off completely flush. The batten acts as a filler to give a clean line, and will be filled and painted with the rest of the bed.

The top edge of the side panels should be rounded over either with a router and a round-over cutter, or by planing and sanding. Alternatively, glue and nail a half-round molding to the top edges for a professional-looking finish.

PADDED HEADBOARD

The padded and upholstered headboard pulls forward to reveal additional storage space at the bed head.

④ Attaching the Headboard Cross Rail in Place
Headboard cross rail is attached with two screws kept low in cross rail.

⑤ Attaching the Triangular Fillers at each Side
Triangular fillers are made from the same material as the side panels, and give a flush finish at each side. Cut the fillers to fit exactly and screw through from the inside of the triangular supports.

⑥ Headboard and Batten
Screw lower headboard section in place. Clamp the strengthening batten to top edge and screw down.

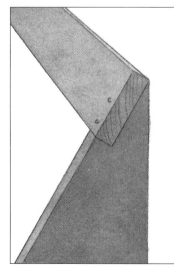

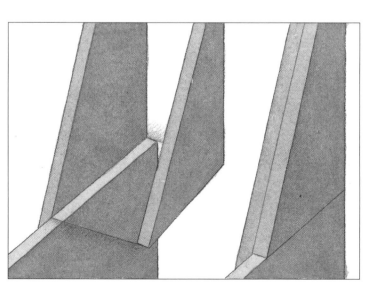

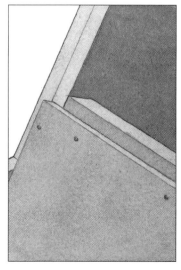

Bed with Trundle Drawer

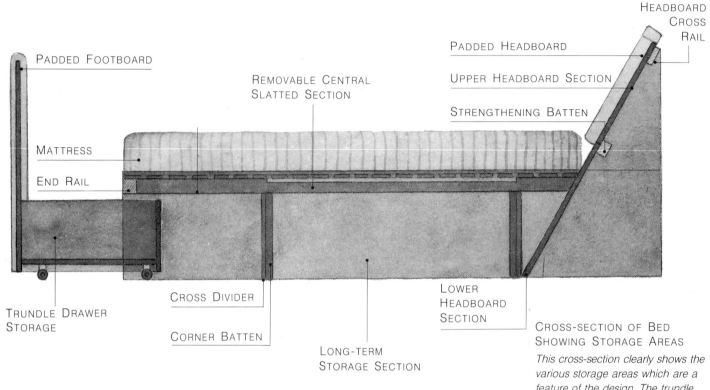

PADDED FOOTBOARD

MATTRESS

END RAIL

TRUNDLE DRAWER STORAGE

CROSS DIVIDER

CORNER BATTEN

REMOVABLE CENTRAL SLATTED SECTION

LONG-TERM STORAGE SECTION

PADDED HEADBOARD

UPPER HEADBOARD SECTION

STRENGTHENING BATTEN

HEADBOARD CROSS RAIL

LOWER HEADBOARD SECTION

CROSS-SECTION OF BED SHOWING STORAGE AREAS
This cross-section clearly shows the various storage areas which are a feature of the design. The trundle drawer is particularly easy to reach.

1 Adding the Filler Piece
Use a piece of softwood to fill the gap between the side and lower headboard section.

2 Attaching the Mattress-support Side Rails in Place
Cut the headboard ends of the mattress-support side rails at an angle to fit neatly against the lower headboard section. Note that the top edge of the side panel is rounded to give a neat finish.

3 Joining the End Rail
End rail is joined to side rails using end-lap joints; end rail laps on top and is screwed to side rails.

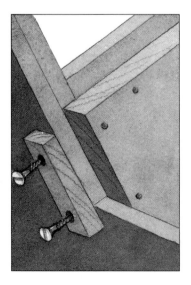

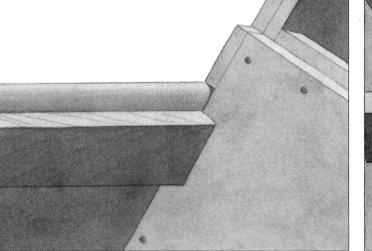

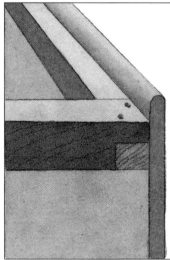

MATTRESS SUPPORT SECTION

The side rails are cut to the length of the mattress, plus a little overlength so that the angle can be cut into the headboard. Place their 2in (50mm) face on the cross dividers alongside the sides, and scribe one end of each rail to the angle of the headboard. Cut this angle and push them against the headboard, then mark them off flush with the ends of the side panels and cut them square.

The end rail is cut to the width of the mattress. Cut end-lap joints *(see* **Techniques, page 86** *)* to join the side and end rails (fig 3).

Glue and screw the side rails in place, screwing through the rails and into the side panels. Fix the end rail in place by inserting small screws through the end-lap joints.

The center rail is cut from 2 × 3in (50 × 75mm) softwood to the length of the mattress plus a little overlength. Rest it on the cross dividers, and scribe to the angle of the headboard, as before. Cut the center rail to length to butt tightly

A unit of the mattress support section (above) lifts out for access to ample but unobtrusive storage space under the bed.

against the inner face of the end rail. Screw it down into the cross dividers.

Drill through the end rail into the end of the center rail in two places, to a depth of between 3–4in (75–100mm) and dry-dowel the joint

using $\frac{1}{2}$in (12mm) doweling *(see* **Techniques, page 90** *)*.

Work out how many slats you need by dividing the length of the mattress by 4in (100mm) – the total of one slat plus a gap. Cut all the

slats to the width of the mattress. The area between the cross dividers is a slatted unit which can be lifted out to give access to storage below.

The softwood cross battens hold the slats together on the slatted unit. Measure the internal distance between the cross dividers and cut four lengths of 1 × 3in (25 × 75mm) to this dimension.

Using a spacing batten *(see* **Techniques, page 80** *)*, space the slats equally and mark the position of the cross battens on to the first slat. The two outermost slats should be positioned in from the ends by the thickness of the side rails – that is, at least 1$\frac{1}{2}$in (38mm). Screw the ends of the outer cross battens in place to the first slat. Continue along the cross battens, spacing and screwing down the rest of the slats. Then space the innermost two cross battens equally in between and screw them in place (fig 5).

Place this panel on the center section and screw the remaining slats into the side rails, spacing them equally. Make sure that there is a slat flush with each end (fig 6).

4 **Joining End and Center Rail**
Center rail butts against end rail. Drill through end rail and hammer dowels in place.

5 **Making the Under-mattress Lift-out Slatted Unit**
The slatted unit between the cross-dividers can be lifted out. Slats are screwed to four cross battens. The outer two cross battens are inset so that they clear the side rails.

6 **Spacing the Fixed Slats**
Place lift-out unit over the center section and screw remaining slats, equally spaced, to side rails.

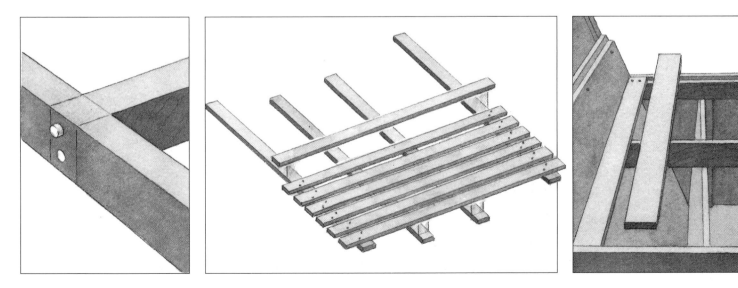

BED WITH TRUNDLE DRAWER

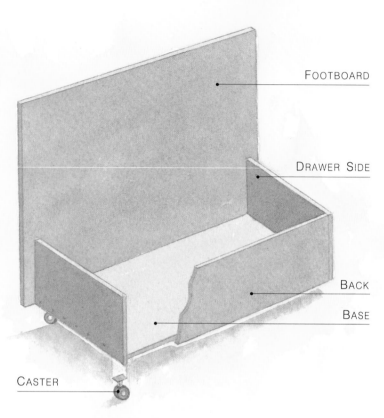

FOOTBOARD

DRAWER SIDE

BACK

BASE

CASTER

of the base around the outside of the carcass. Finally, screw 2in (50mm) casters to the four corners of the base to allow easy movement.

UPHOLSTERY FOR THE BED

THE PADDING

The padding is expanded-polysty-rene foam of three different thicknesses, covered with Dacron. Cut the foam with an electric carving knife or any blade with a serrated edge.

HEADBOARD

Cut a piece of 2in (50mm) foam to the size of the headboard's upper section. Spray one face of the head-board with latex spray adhesive and stick the foam to it, smoothing it down carefully.

Cut a piece of 2in (50mm) foam to the length of the top edge and stick it in place, positioning it care-fully, with spray adhesive.

Use 1in (25mm) foam for the sides. Cut two pieces, each to the

length of the headboard's side, plus the thickness of the foam covering the top, and stick one on each side.

Stick a thin layer of Dacron over all the foam with the spray adhesive and leave to dry.

FOOTBOARD

Cut one piece of 1in (25mm) foam to the width of the footboard, to run from the top of the drawer sides up and over the top of the footboard and down to the bottom edge.

Draw a line on the inside face of the footboard in line with the top of the drawer sides and spray adhesive on the wood down to this line, and on to the outside face.

Stick down the foam, starting at the line and smoothing it on to the wood. Ease it over the top and down the other side of the footboard.

Cut two pieces of 1in (25mm) foam to fit the small sections either side of the drawer, on the inside face of the footboard, and stick in place as shown (fig 3).

Cut two pieces of $\frac{1}{2}$in (12mm) foam to the size of the side edges and stick one to each edge.

---

① Trundle Drawer Assembly
Note that sides are set in from the footboard and that the back sits within the sides.

THE TRUNDLE DRAWER

The bed should be finished before you make the drawer. The foot-board is cut from one piece of MDF to $\frac{1}{2}$in (12mm) less than the overall width of the bed. Its height is as required – ours is 35in (890mm).

Preferably, the height of the two MDF drawer sides should be at least 6in (150mm) lower than the sides of the bed. This allows the drawer to run underneath the end rail and accommodates casters. Our sides are therefore 12in (300mm). The length is 24in (610mm).

For the back, cut one piece of

MDF to the height of the drawer sides. Its width should be that of the mattress minus 2in (50mm). Glue and screw through the sides into the back edges, then glue and screw through the footboard into the sides, ensuring that the footboard over-laps the sides equally.

Measure the internal dimensions of the rectangle for the size of the drawer base, and cut it to size from MDF. The base should be spaced 1in (25mm) up from the bottom edges of the sides and back. To fit it firmly in place for screwing, lay the base on scrap battens 1in (25mm) thick, then place the carcass over the base. This will ensure an even 1in (25mm) spacing up from the bot-tom edges of the carcass.

Screw through into the edges of the base on all four sides, having marked the height of the center line

---

② Padding the Headboard
Stick 2in (50mm) thick foam to upper headboard section and top edge; 1in (25mm) foam at sides.

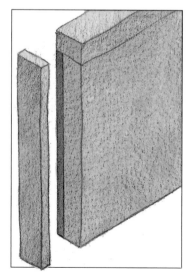

③ Padding the Footboard
One piece of 1in (25mm) foam covers front/back of footboard, plus 1in (12mm) foam at sides.

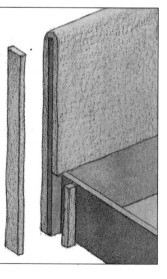

Put a layer of Dacron over the foam, stick in place and leave to dry.

THE COVERS

The bottom edges of the covers are folded under and joined to the bases of the padded headboard and footboard with Velcro to allow easy removal for cleaning.

If you use a large-patterned fabric you will need to piece together three same-sized widths of fabric, and match the pattern along the seams. Plain fabrics are simpler to use, since no pattern-matching is necessary and you can use one long length of fabric rather than three widths to cover the large area.

If you lack the confidence to make separate border panels to go around the sides of the covers, you can achieve good results by skipping that step and joining the front panel directly to the back panel.

HEADBOARD COVER

Cut two panels – one for the front and one for the back of the padded headboard, allowing extra fabric at the edges for the seams. If you are

piecing together widths, cut them oversized (allowing extra fabric for internal as well as edge seams) and match the internal seam positions of the front and back panels.

Fold the front and back panels in half across their width and make a notch at the center of each top edge, to match up the front, border, and back panels later when sewing.

Next, measure for the long border panel that will go around the top and sides and under the bottom edge by 3in (75mm). Cut the border panel, allowing extra fabric on each side for the seams, and then fold it in half widthways and make notches on both edges – in the center and where the panel corners will be.

With right sides together, place the edge of the front panel to the edge of the border panel, matching the notches. Pin, baste, and then machine-stitch the seam, working from the center notch outwards, first in one direction and then the other, along the top and down each side until you reach the bottom corners; this ensures that the panels are sewn together evenly.

Attach the back panel to the other edge of the border panel, right sides together and with notches and corners matching. Pin, baste, and machine-stitch as before, down to each bottom corner.

Hem by machine all the remaining edges of the cover. Cut a strip of Velcro to the length of the long panels and machine-stitch it in place to the bottom edges of the front and back panels, so that the bottom edge of the front panel wraps around to the back panel. Fold in the two border pieces first, and join the panel flaps together with the Velcro for a neat finish.

FOOTBOARD COVER

Measure the padded footboard from edge to edge and cut one panel for the inside face, allowing extra all round for the edge seams, plus about 3in (75mm) at the bottom to enclose the padding. If piecing together widths, follow instructions for headboard cover for extra seam allowances. Cut the panel for the outside face, allowing extra fabric all round for edge seams

plus enough at the bottom to fold the edge under. Cut the material for the long border, allowing extra fabric for the edge seams and for folding under the bottom edge.

Make the cover as for the headboard cover and attach the outside panel to the border panel. For the inside panel, sew down as far as the drawer sides, then attach a small piece of fabric on each side to cover the narrow border on either side of the drawer. Machine-stitch these pieces to the cover with right sides together. Cut the fabric so that it fits neatly around each drawer side turning the edges under and then machine-stitching. Turn under all the bottom edges and machine-stitch.

On the outside, fold in the ends and hem along the bottom edge. Fit the bottom edge to the footboard with Velcro, using the soft part on the fabric and the hard part on the wood. To attach Velcro to the wood, glue, nail, or staple it in place, or use self-adhesive Velcro.

On the inside face, secure the bottom edge and side flaps to the footboard with Velcro as before.

4 **Making the Cover for the Headboard**

Cut the front and back panels allowing extra fabric all around for seams and (if necessary) piecing together widths, plus about 3in (75mm) to fold under the bottom edge. Pin, baste, then machine-stitch seams.

5 **Making the Cover for the Footboard**

Make up as for the headboard, carefully cutting and fitting around drawer sides. At the narrow sides of the drawer, attach thin strips of fabric. Secure with Velcro along the bottom edge and along side flaps.

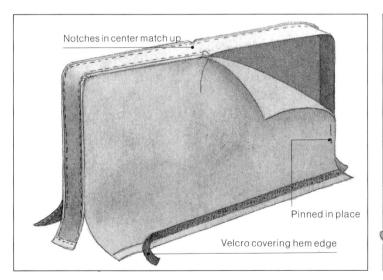

Notches in center match up

Pinned in place

Velcro covering hem edge

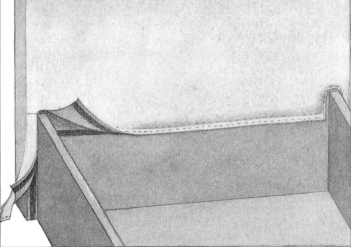

Tools

Adhesive spreader These are palm-size pieces of semi-flexible plastic with serrated or notched edges which are used to spread adhesives over wide surfaces, evenly, and at the correct rate. Because the size of the serrations or notches affects the spreading rate, adhesive manufacturers usually supply a spreader with their adhesives for brands where a spreader is required: mainly contact-types and tiling and flooring adhesives.

Bench stop and vise A woodwork vise is fitted to the underside of a bench, with the jaws level with the bench top. The jaws are lined and topped with hardwood to protect the work and any tools being used. Some vises also incorporate a small steel peg (a "dog") that can be raised above the main jaw level. This allows awkward or long pieces of wood to be clamped in position when used with a bench stop which is fixed at the opposite end of the bench stop.

Sliding bevel (1) Also called a bevel gauge, this is a type of square used to mark out lumber at any required angle. The sliding blade can be locked against the stock by means of a locking lever and the blade can form any angle with the stock.

Marking gauge (2) Essential for setting out woodworking joints, this is used to mark both widths and thicknesses with only a light scratch. The gauge comprises a handle, on which slides a stock bearing a steel marking pin. This movable stock can be locked in any position with a thumb screw so the steel pin is fixed at a precise point.

Mortise gauge (3) Similar to a marking gauge, it has two pins – one fixed, one adjustable – to mark out both sides of a mortise at the same time. Some types have an additional pin fixed below the beam so that the tool can be used as a marking gauge.

Contour gauge This is also called a shape tracer or a scribing gauge. It comprises a row of steel pins or plastic fingers held in a central bar. When pressed against an object, like a baseboard, the pins follow the shape of the object.

Utility knife A razor-sharp blade which is used to score a thin, accurate line for a saw or chisel to follow, ensuring a precise cut. The flat face of the knife can be run against the blade of a try square or straight-edge. A paring chisel is placed in the knife line for accurate paring of the last cut.

Miter box A simple open-topped wooden box which is used to guide saws into material at a fixed 45° or 90° angle, to ensure a square cut.

Plumb bob and chalk A plumb line is used to check verticals and mark accurate vertical lines, in chalk, on walls. A plumb bob is simply a pointed weight attached to a long length of string. Before use, the string can be rubbed with a stick of colored chalk. Hold the string in the required position at the top, wait for the plumb bob to stop swinging, then carefully press the string against the wall at the bottom and then pluck the string to leave a line on the wall. Most hardware stores stock chalk lines (plumb bobs with line winders and powdered chalk containers): these save time by automatically dusting the line with chalk as it is withdrawn.

Portable workbench A collapsible, portable workbench is vital for woodworking. A large, fixed workbench in a garage or shed is important, but the major advantage of the portable type is that it is lightweight and can be carried to the job, where it provides sturdy support when final adjustments have to be made.

A portable bench is like a giant vise – the worksurface comprises two sections which can be opened wide or closed tightly according to the dimensions of the work and the nature of the task. It can hold large and awkward objects.

Scribing block To fit an item neatly against a wall (which is very unlikely to be perfectly flat) the item has to be "scribed" flat to the wall using a small block of wood and a pencil (*see **Techniques, page 91**). A scribing block is simply an offcut of wood measuring about 1in x 1in x 1in (25mm x 25mm x 25mm). The block is held against the wall, a sharp pencil is held against the opposite end of the block, and the block and the pencil are moved in a unit along the wall to mark a line on the item to be fitted. If you cut to this line, the item will then fit tightly against the wall.

Carpenter's level (9) Used for checking that surfaces are horizontal or vertical. A 24in (610mm) long level is the most useful all-round size. An aluminum or steel level will withstand knocks and it can be either I-girder or box-shaped in section. Ideally, a 9in (225mm) "torpedo" carpenter's level is also useful to have, for working in confined spaces such as alcoves and inside cupboards. It may be used in conjunction with a straight-edge over longer surfaces.

Steel measuring tape A 12ft (3.6m) or 18ft (5.5m) long, lockable tape (metal or plastic) is best, and one with a window in the casing that makes it easier to read measurements.

Steel bench rule Since the rule is made of steel, the graduations are very precise and indelible. A rule graduated on both sides in imperial and metric is the most useful. The rule can also serve as a precise straight-edge for marking cutting lines.

Straight-edge Can be made from a piece of 1 x 2in (25 x 50mm) scrap wood. It is used to tell whether a surface is flat and also for checking whether two points are aligned with each other.

Try square (4) An L-shaped precision tool comprising a steel blade and stock (or handle) set at a perfect right angle to each other on both

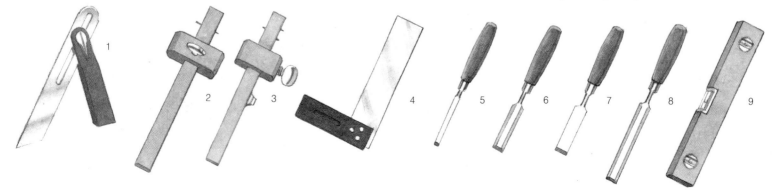

the inside and outside edges. Used for marking cutting lines at right angles to an edge and for checking a square.

SUPPLEMENTARY TOOLS

Drill stand Enables a power drill to be used with extreme accuracy when, for example, joining doweling (*see* **Techniques, page 90**). The hole will be perpendicular to the surface and its depth can be carefully controlled. The drill is lowered on to the work with a spring-loaded lever which gives good control and accuracy.

Metal detector Pinpoints metal objects such as electric cables and water and gas pipes hidden in walls, ceilings, and floors. Electronically operated, it buzzes or flashes when metal is found.

TOOLS FOR SHARPENING AND CUTTING

Chisels Used to cut slots in wood or to pare off thin slivers. Some chisels may be used with a mallet when cutting slots. When new, a chisel's cutting edge is ground and must be honed with an oilstone to sharpen it.
Mortise chisel (5) Used with a mallet for cutting deep slots.
Bench chisel (6) Used for undercutting in confined spaces, such as when making dovetail joints.
Firmer chisel (7) For general-purpose use around the home.
Paring chisel (8) Has a long blade for cutting deep joints or long grooves.

Doweling jig A simple doweling jig clamps on to a piece of work, ensuring that the drill is aligned accurately over the center of the dowel hole to be drilled. It also guides the drill vertically.

DRILLS

Hand drill (10) For drilling holes for screws or for making large holes, particularly in wood. It will

make holes in metal and is useful where there is no power source. A handle attached to a toothed wheel is used to turn the drill in its chuck.
Power drill (11) These range from a simple, single-speed model (which will drill holes only in soft materials) to a multi-speed drill with electronic control. Most jobs call for something in between the two, such as a two-speed drill with hammer action. The two speeds enable most hard materials to be drilled and the hammer action means that you can also drill into the hardest walls.

DRILL BITS

You will need a selection of twist bits in various sizes and of different types for wood and metal, for use with a drill.

Brad-point bit (12) Used to make dowel holes in wood. The tip has two cutting spurs on the side and a center point to prevent the bit from wandering off center. Diameters range from $\frac{1}{8}$in (3mm) to $\frac{1}{2}$in (12mm).
Twist drill bit (13) Used with an electric drill for drilling small holes in wood and metal. Carbon-steel drills are for wood only: drilling into metal requires a high-speed steel drill.
Masonry bit (14) Has a specially hardened tungsten-carbide tip for drilling into masonry to the exact size required for an anchor. Special percussion drill bits are available for use with a hammer drill when boring into concrete.
Countersink bit (15) After a hole is drilled in wood, a countersink bit is used to cut a recess for the screwhead to sit in, so ensuring that it lies below the surface. Different types are available for use with a carpenter's brace and an electric drill. Head diameters are $\frac{3}{8}$in (9mm), $\frac{1}{2}$in (12mm), and $\frac{9}{16}$in (15mm). Carbon-steel bits can be used for wood, but high-speed steel bits can be used for wood, plastic, or metal.
Spade bit (16) Is used with an electric drill. It has a point at the end of the shank and its flat shank end allows it to slot into the drill chuck. Diameters are from $\frac{1}{4}$in (6mm) to $1\frac{1}{2}$in (38mm). For maxi-

mum efficiency the bit must be turned at high speed from about 1000 to 2000 rpm. It can be used to drill into cross grain, end grain, and manmade boards. Also known as a speedbore bit.
Auger bit (17) Has a tapered, square shank that fits into a carpenter's brace. It is used to make deep holes in wood, the usual lengths being up to 10in (250mm). Diameters range from $\frac{1}{4}$in (6mm) to $1\frac{1}{2}$in (38mm). The tip has a screw thread to draw the bit into the wood.
Forstner bit (18) A Forstner bit, or hinge-sinker bit, is primarily used for boring $1\frac{3}{8}$in (35mm) or 1in (25mm) diameter flat bottomed holes in cabinet and wardrobe doors to accept the hinge bosses on concealed hinges. Forstner bits are used in electric drills, ideally fitted in drill stands, and set to drill no deeper than $\frac{1}{2}$in (12mm).

Oilstone and honing guide The first sharpens and the second maintains the correct angle for sharpening chisel and plane blades. An oilstone is a rectangular block of stone with grit on both sides. Oil is used as a lubricant while the blade is being sharpened on the stone, so you will need a can of fine oil nearby.

The honing guide is an inexpensive tool which makes sharpening easier and more efficient. The blade of the tool to be sharpened is inserted at an angle and clamped in place, then the guide is repeatedly rolled back and forth on the surface of the oilstone.

Power router (19) This portable electric tool is used to cut grooves, recesses, and many types of joints in lumber, as well as to shape the edges of long lumber battens to form decorative moldings. A whole range of cutting bits in different shapes and sizes is available and when fitted into the router the bits revolve at very high speed (about 25,000 rpm) to cut the wood smoothly and cleanly (20). Although hand routers (which look like small planes) are available, whenever routers are referred to in this book, it is the power router to which the remarks are directed.

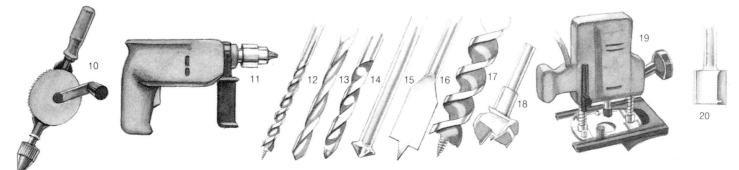

TOOLS

SAWS

Circular saw (1) Invaluable for cutting large pieces of lumber or sheets of board. It will also cut grooves and angles. The most popular size has a diameter of $7\frac{1}{4}$in (184mm). Circular saws can be extremely dangerous and must be used carefully. The piece of work must be held securely and the blade depth set so that it will not cut into anything below the work. The tool should be fitted with an upper and lower blade guard. Support your work on scrap battens to avoid cutting into work-benches or floors.

Coping saw (2) Used to make curved or circular cuts. It has a narrow blade, which can be swiveled. When cutting, the blade can be angled as necessary so that the frame clears the edge of the work. Drill a hole close to the edge of the piece to be cut out, and thread the coping saw blade through the hole before reconnecting it to the handle and starting to cut.

Dovetail saw (3) Also called a gent's saw. This fine-tooth form of back saw with a stiffened back is ideal for making delicate and precise saw cuts. It is particularly useful for making dovetail joints.

Hand saws (4) Are used for rough cutting rather than fine carpentry. They have a flexible blade of 20–26in (510–670mm) in length, and a wooden or plastic handle. They are useful for general-purpose cutting of wood and fiberboards.

Saber saw (7) Will cut a variety of materials, and is much more versatile than a circular saw, although not as quick or powerful. It also cuts curves, shapes, angles, and holes in the middle of panels. The best models offer variable speeds – slow for hard materials and fast for soft. The latest models have either a reciprocating or a pendulum action. In these cases the blade goes backwards and forwards as well as up and down, which allows for much faster cutting on straight lines.

Compass saw (5) Also called a keyhole saw, it is designed to cut holes and shapes in wood. It has a narrow, tapered blade which will cut keyholes, for example. A hole is first drilled and the saw blade inserted to make the cut. Compass saws are useful for cutting holes for inset sinks where a power Saber saw is not available.

Back saw (6) For cutting the tenon part of a mortise and tenon joint (see **Techniques, page 88**), and also useful for other delicate and accurate work. It has a stiffened back and the blade is about 10–12in (250–300mm) long.

Surforms Available in a range of lengths from approximately 6–10in (150–250mm), these rasps are useful for the initial shaping of wood. However, further fine finishing by hand is needed to obtain a smooth surface. The steel blade has a pattern of alternating small teeth and holes through which waste wood passes, so that the teeth do not get clogged up. When blunt, the blade is simply replaced.

SUPPLEMENTARY TOOLS

Hacksaw For cutting metal. A traditional hacksaw has a wooden handle and a solid metal frame. The blade is tensioned by a wing-nut. Modern hacksaws have a tubular frame which is adjustable for different lengths of blade. A "junior" hacksaw is ideal for sawing small items or for working in confined spaces.

HANDS TOOLS

Awl Used to make a small pilot hole in wood to take a screw. It is twisted into the wood with a continuous circular movement.

CLAMPS

For securing glued pieces of work while they are setting. There are many types of clamp, but the C-clamp is the most commonly used and is available in a wide range of jaw sizes.

Folding wedges are sometimes useful for securing an object while it is being glued. You can make two by cutting diagonally through a block of wood. For instructions on how to make and use folding wedges, see page 81.

Bar clamps These employ a long metal bar, and are indispensable for holding together large frameworks. Initially, rent rather than buy bar clamps, although you can improvise in some cases by making a rope tourniquet. This consists of a piece of rope which is tied around the object and a length of stick to twist the rope and so clamp the frame tightly.

Band clamp A nylon webbing clamp to apply even pressure around frames when they are being assembled. The webbing, like narrow seat-belt type material, is looped around the frame, pulled as tight as possible by hand, and then finally tightened by means of a screw mechanism or ratchet winder. Band clamps are cheaper alternatives to bar clamps.

C-clamp Also called a frame clamp or fast-action clamp, it is important for our projects that the jaws of the clamp open at least 8in (200mm). The lumber to be held in the clamp is placed between the jaws which are then tightened by turning a thumb-screw, tommy bar, or other type of handle. In the case of the fast-action clamp, one jaw is free to slide on a bar, and after sliding this jaw up to the workpiece, final tightening is achieved by turning the handle. In all cases, to prevent damage to the workpiece, scraps of wood are placed between it and the jaws of the clamp.

HAMMERS

Claw hammer (9) The claw side of the head of the hammer is used to extract nails from a piece of work quickly and cleanly.

Cross-peen hammer (10) The peen is the tapered section opposite the flat hammer head, and it is used for starting off small brads and tacks held in the fingers.

Tack hammer A smaller version of the cross-peen, this is useful for light work.

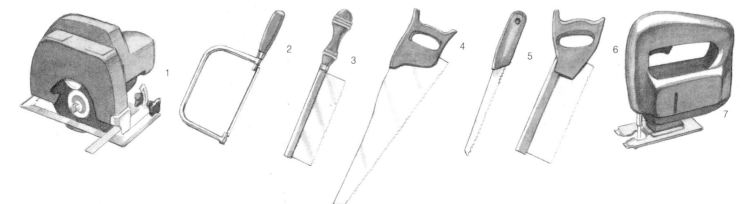

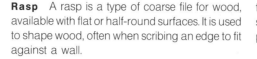
Mallet Most commonly used to strike mortise chisels, although if a chisel has an impact-resistant handle then a hammer may also be used. The tapered wooden head ensures square contact with the object being struck.

Nailset Used with a hammer to drive nails and brads below the surface so that they are hidden; the hole can then be filled. The pointed end is "cupped" to fit neatly over a nail or brad head.

Orbital sander Otherwise known as a finishing sander, this gives a fine, smooth surface finish to wood. A gritted sanding sheet is fitted to the sander's base plate. Sheets are graded from coarse to fine, and the grade used depends on the roughness of the surface to be sanded. Orbital sanders produce a great deal of dust, so always wear a mask when using one.

Pliers Used to remove nails and tacks from wood. The bevel-edged jaws grip the nail close to the surface of the wood, and the pliers are rocked back and forth to extract it.

PLANES

Smoothing plane (11) A general-purpose, hand-held plane for smoothing and straightening surfaces and edges. The plane is about 10in (250mm) long and its blade 2–2$\frac{1}{4}$in (50–60mm) wide. The wider the blade the better the finish on wide lumber. There is a fine adjustment for depth of cut and a lever for lateral adjustment.

Block plane (12) Held in the palm of the hand, it is easy to use for small work and beveling edges. Also useful for planing end grain.

Jack plane (13) Longer than a smoothing plane, it is used for straightening long edges and is a good all-purpose plane.

Power plane (14) Finishes lumber to precise dimensions. A one-hand model is lightweight and can be used anywhere, whereas the heavier two-hander is intended for workbench use. A power plane will also cut bevels and rabbets.

Rasp A rasp is a type of coarse file for wood, available with flat or half-round surfaces. It is used to shape wood, often when scribing an edge to fit against a wall.

Sanding block and sanding paper A sanding block is used with sanding paper to finish and smooth flat surfaces. The block is made of cork, rubber, or softwood and the sanding paper is wrapped around it. Make sure in doing so that the paper is not wrinkled. Sanding paper used without a block tends to produce an uneven surface. Sheets of sanding paper are graded from coarse to fine and are selected according to the roughness of the surface to be sanded. Coarse paper is used for a very rough surface and fine paper for finishing.

Screwdrivers There is no single type of screwdriver that is better than the rest; personal preference is what matters. They come in many shapes and sizes, and the main differences are the type of tip (for slotted or Phillips screws), the length, and the shape of the handle, which varies from straight or fluted to bulb-shaped. Phillips screwdrivers can be used on most Phillips screws but certain speciality recess screws require their own special screwdrivers.

Ideally, you should have a range of screwdrivers for dealing with all sizes of screws. Ratchet models, which return the handle to its starting point, are easy to operate since your hand grip does not need to change. The spiral action screwdriver is very efficient (though very expensive) and it works like a bicycle pump rather than by turning the handle.

Cordless screwdriver A fairly new tool, it is expensive but can save much time and effort. Mainly used for Phillips screws.

SUPPLEMENTARY TOOLS

Metal file Gives a metal edge the required shape and finish. Most files are supplied with a removable handle which can be transferred to a file of a different size. A flat or half-round file (one side flat, the other curved) are good general-purpose tools.

Hand staple gun A trigger-operated tool which fires a staple straight into a surface, usually fabric, fiberboard, or thin wood over a wooden batten. Its advantage over conventional nailing with a hammer is that, as it is used one-handed, the other hand is free to hold the work.

Power staple gun Easier to fire. Fires heavy-duty staples into thicker surfaces, such as ceilings. It is preferable to buy the same brand of gun and staples to prevent jamming.

Paintbrushes A set of paintbrushes for painting and varnishing should ideally comprise three sizes – 1in (25mm), 2in (50mm), and 3in (75mm). A better finish is always achieved by matching the size of brush to the surface – a small brush for narrow surfaces, a large brush for wide areas. Always clean thoroughly after use.

Electric paint sprayer Can produce a very smooth finish once its use is mastered. It may be preferable to hire rather than buy one – initially at least – since airless spray guns and compressors are expensive. Always work parallel to the surface you are spraying, applying two thin coats of paint rather than one thick coat.

Wrench A wrench is required for tightening carriage bolts, and any type that fits the head of the bolt is suitable. If the correct-size open-ended or ring wrench is not available, any type of adjustable wrench may be used.

Caulking gun Used to eject a bead of mastic-type waterproofing sealants (or caulking) into gaps where water might penetrate, such as around shower trays. A cartridge of caulking or sealant is held in the frame (or "gun"), and a plunger, pushes the caulking out of a nozzle at the end of the cartridge.

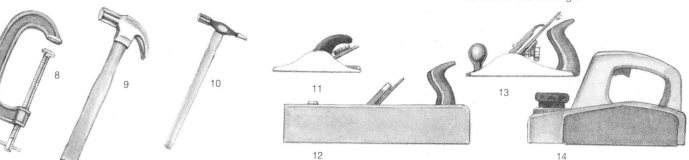

8   9   10   11   12   13   14

MATERIALS

LUMBER

Lumber is classified into two groups – softwoods and hardwoods. Softwoods come from evergreen trees and hardwoods from deciduous trees. Avoid wood which is badly cracked or split, although you need not worry about fine, surface cracks since these can be planed, sanded, or filled. Do not buy warped wood, as it will be impossible to work with.

When you get your wood home, condition it for about ten days. As the wood will have been stored in the open air at the yard, it will be "wet". To avoid warping and aid drying, stack boards in a pile, with offcuts of wood placed between each board to allow air to circulate. This will condition the wood, ready for use.

Softwood Softwood is much less expensive than hardwood and is used in general building work. Softwood is sold either by the *lineal* foot or the *board* foot. The former is based on the length of a piece of wood – for example, 8ft of 1 by 2 (1×2in [25×50mm]). The board foot is calculated by the thickness in inches $\times$ width in feet $\times$ length in feet – for example, 10ft of 1 by 6 would be 5 board feet: 1in $\times \frac{1}{2}$ft (6in) $\times$ 10ft.

The smooth wood used for the projects in this book, for which appearance and accuracy are important, will need to have been planed. This is the state in which softwood is commonly sold in local lumberyards; in the trade it is referred to as "S4S" (smooth 4 sides), and, since planing takes a little off each face, planed softwood is $\frac{1}{4}-\frac{3}{8}$in (6–9mm) smaller in width and thickness than its stated size. Sizes should only be thought of as rough guides rather than exact measurements.

Hardwood Expensive and not as easy to obtain as softwoods, hardwoods often have to be ordered or bought from a specialist lumberyard. In home woodwork, hardwood is usually confined to moldings and beadings, which are used to give exposed sawn edges a neat finish.

SHEET MATERIAL BOARDS

Sheet material boards are mechanically made from wood and other fibers. They are versatile, relatively inexpensive, made to uniform quality, and are available in large sheets. Sheet materials are graded according to the quality of finished surfaces and are made in sheets of 4×8ft (1220×2440mm). Most stockists will saw them to the size you require.

Hardboard Also called masonite, and the best known fiberboard. Common thicknesses are $\frac{1}{8}$in, $\frac{3}{16}$in, and $\frac{1}{4}$in (3mm, 4mm, and 6mm). As hardboard is weak and has to be supported on a framework, it is mainly used for paneling. Denser types of tempered hardboard can be used for cladding partitions; softer types for bulletin boards.

Medium-density fiberboard (MDF) A good, highly compressed, general-purpose building board. You may find that it has to be ordered from a plywood wholesaler (your retail yard can do this for you), but it is worth it since it does not flake or splinter when cut, and leaves a clean, hard-sawn edge. It also takes a very good paint finish, even on its edges. Thicknesses range from around $\frac{3}{16}$in to $1\frac{3}{8}$in (5mm to 35mm).

Particleboard Made by binding wood chips together under pressure, it is rigid, dense, and fairly heavy. Particleboard is strong when reasonably well supported, but sawing it can leave an unstable edge and can also quickly blunt a saw. Ordinary screws do not hold well in particleboard, and it is best to use twin-threaded screws *(see* **Screws, page 79** *)*. The most common thicknesses are $\frac{1}{2}$in, $\frac{3}{4}$in, and 1in (12mm, 19mm, and 25mm). The better-quality laminated boards are far stronger than plain particleboard.

Plywood Made by gluing thin wood veneers together in plies (layers) with the grain in each ply running at right angles to that of its neighbors. This gives the board strength and helps prevent warping. Plywood is graded for quality, taking into account the amount of knots and surface markings present: N is perfect, followed by A, B, C, and D in decreasing order of quality; D is for rough work only. AC or ACX (the "X" stands for exterior) denotes A grade on one side and C on the other, and is a good, economical option where only one side will be visible.

Plywood is available with a range of surface veneers such as teak or mahogany, or with a plastic finish. Common thicknesses are $\frac{1}{8}$in, $\frac{1}{4}$in, $\frac{1}{2}$in, and $\frac{3}{4}$in (3mm, 6mm, 12mm, and 19mm).

Lumber core Made by sandwiching natural lumber strips between wood veneers, the latter usually of Far Eastern redwood or plain birch. Although plain birch is a little more expensive than redwood, it is of a much better quality. Lumber core is very strong, but can leave an ugly edge when sawn, making edge fixings difficult. It is graded in the same way as plywood and common thicknesses are $\frac{1}{2}$in, $\frac{3}{4}$in, and 1in (12mm, 19mm, and 25mm). It is very rigid, and therefore ideal for a long span of shelving.

Tongued-and-grooved boards Widely used for cladding frameworks and walls. Each board has a tongue on one side and a slot on the other side. The tongue fits into the slot on the adjacent board to form an area of cladding; this expands and contracts according to temperature and humidity without cracks opening up between boards.

Ordinary tongued-and-grooved boards fit together like floorboards, but tongued-and-grooved boards for cladding have some form of decoration; this can be a beaded joint, or a beveled edge which forms the attractive V-joint of tongued, grooved, and V-jointed (TGV) boards.

ADHESIVES

Adhesives For all general indoor woodworking, use an aliphatic resin glue (yellow woodworker's glue) – all glue manufacturers produce their own brands. Use a two part resorcinol glue (guaranteed waterproof) in areas where there may be water splashing or condensation. If joints do not meet perfectly, use a gap-filling adhesive. Ceramic tiles require their own special adhesive (of a thick, buttery consistency) which is supplied, ready mixed, in tubs.

FINISHES

Paint A liquid gloss (oil-based) paint is suitable for wood, and is applied after a suitable undercoat. Generally, two thin coats of gloss are better than one thick coat. Non-drip gloss paint is an alternative. It has a jelly-like consistency and does not require an undercoat, although a quality finish may need a second coat. Use a liquid gloss if you want to spray paint.

Varnish Normally applied by brush, varnish can also be sprayed on. It is available as a gloss, satin, or matte finish, all clear. However, varnish also comes in a range of colors, so that you can change the color of the wood and protect it simultaneously. The color does not sink into the wood, so that if the surface becomes scratched or marked then its original color will show through. For this reason, a wood stain or dye is sometimes used to change the color of wood. It sinks into the wood, but offers no protection, so a varnish or clear lacquer will also be needed.

Moldings   Wood moldings are used as ornamentation and to cover gaps or fixings in a wooden construction. The term "molding" encompasses everything from a simple, thin edge-banding to architraves and baseboards. A variety of shaped cutters produce many different shapes and sizes. In the unlikely event of your being unable to buy the shape of molding you want, you could make your own using a router.

Battens   A general term used to describe a narrow strip of wood. The usual sizes are 1 × 1in (25 × 25mm) or 1 × 2in (25 × 50mm).

Battens serve one of two main functions. They can be screwed to a wall to serve as bearers for shelves. Alternatively, they can be fixed in a framework on a wall, with sheet material or boards mounted over them to form a new "wall".

Dowels   Used to make framework joints or to join boards edge-to-edge or edge-to-face.

Hardwood dowels are sold in diameters of $\frac{1}{4}$in, $\frac{3}{8}$in, and $\frac{1}{2}$in (6mm, 9mm, and 12mm). You can buy packs of dowels cut to length (either 1in or 1$\frac{1}{2}$in [25mm or 38mm]), or you can buy long lengths and cut them to size. Generally speaking, dowel lengths should be about one-and-a-half times the thickness of the boards being joined.

NAILS

Nails are generally sold by their penny (or "d") size. The most common are 2d (1in), 4d (1$\frac{1}{2}$in), 6d (2in), 8d (2$\frac{1}{2}$in), and 10d (3in).

Common nails   With large, flat, circular heads, these are used for strong joints where frames will be covered, and the nails will be hidden.

Annular threaded nails   Used where really strong attachments are required.

Round finishing nails   Used when the finished appearance is important. The heads of these nails are driven flush with the wood's surface or countersunk so they are unobtrusive.

Brads   For attaching thin panels. These have tiny, unobtrusive heads that can be driven in flush with the wood's surface or punched below it.

Hardboard pins   These have deep-drive diamond-shaped heads that sink into the surface – ideal for securing hardboard and other boards to lumber in areas subject to condensation.

Masonry nails   For securing battens to walls as an alternative to screwing and anchoring.

SCREWS

All types of screws are available with either conventional slotted or with Phillips heads. The latter look neat and are the best type to use if you are inserting screws with an electric screwdriver.

For most purposes, screws with flat heads are ideal as, when countersunk, the head lies flush with the surface after insertion. Round-head screws are used for attaching metal fixtures such as shelf brackets and door bolts, which have punched-out rather than countersunk screw holes. Ovalhead screws are often used where a neat appearance is important.

Wood screws   These have a length of smooth shank below the head. When joining two pieces of wood, this produces a strong clamping effect as the screw is tightened, but there is a possibility of the unthreaded shank splitting the wood.

Twin-threaded screws   Quicker to insert than ordinary wood screws and less likely to split wood. Except for larger sizes, they are threaded along their entire length, giving an excellent grip in wood, and also in fiberboard, particleboard, lumber core, and plywood.

WALL FIXTURES AND BOLTS

The choice of wall fixture depends on the type of wall and the weight of the object being attached.

Anchors   Use a masonry drill bit to drill a hole which matches the size of screw being used (a No 10 bit with a No 10 screw, for example). Insert the anchor in the hole, then insert the screw through the object being fitted and into the anchor. Tighten the screw for a secure attachment.

Solid wall fixtures   The method of attaching to a solid brick or block wall is to use an anchor. Anchors will accept a range of screw sizes, typically from No 8 to No 12.

Stud wall fixtures   To guarantee a secure fixture, you should locate the lumber uprights (studs) which form the framework of the wall and drive screws into them. If you want to attach something heavy and the lumber uprights are not in the required position, then you must attach horizontal battens to the lumber uprights, since otherwise the fitting will be unsafe.

Cavity-wall fixtures   Used on hollow walls, which are constructed from wallboard partition or lath and plaster. There are many types of these fixtures, and nearly all of them work on the same principle: expanding wings open up to grip the back of the wallboard or lath and plaster, securing the attachment.

Wall anchor bolt   For heavier objects, a more robust attachment using a wall anchor bolt is advisable. It is similar to an anchor in principle, but has its own heavy-duty machine screw. You need to make a much larger hole in the wall, typically $\frac{3}{8}$in (10mm) in diameter.

LATCHES

Magnetic catches   Most useful on smaller doors which are unlikely to warp. There must be perfect contact between the magnet fitted to the cabinet frame and the strike plate which is fitted to the door. The other important factor is the pulling power of the magnet – on small cabinet doors a "pull" of 4$\frac{1}{2}$–6$\frac{1}{2}$lb (2–3kg) is sufficient. On wardrobe doors a 11–13lb (5–6kg) "pull" is needed.

Mechanical latches   Common types are the spring-loaded ball catch and the roller catch. Again, alignment is vital to success, which is why adjustable types are favored.

SLIDING DOOR TRACKS

Top-hung track   Small tongued sliders or adjustable wheel hangers attached to the top edge of the door sit in the track. Small guides keep the bottom edges of the door aligned.

Bottom-roller track   The door slides on small rollers located in the track. Guides attached at the top of the door keep it aligned in the track.

TILES

Ceramic tiles   There is an enormous range of tiles available, and prices vary according to size, shape, design, and the purpose for which they are required: floor tiles need to be much stronger than decorative wall tiles. The most common sizes are 4$\frac{1}{4}$ × 4$\frac{1}{4}$in (108 × 108mm) and 6 × 6in (150 × 150mm), but rectangular shapes are also now widely available.

After calculating the number of tiles required, allow a few extra to cover breakages. Unless you are using only one box, do not use the tiles straight from the box – mix them up with other boxes to disguise any slight color variations.

TECHNIQUES: SAWING AND CUTTING

WOOD

Wood is available either sawn or planed. Sawn wood is rough in appearance, but is close in width and thickness to the dimensions you specify when ordering. Planed wood is smoothed on all sides, but planing removes $\frac{1}{4}$–$\frac{3}{4}$in (6–19mm) from both the nominal width and the thickness. Sawn wood is ideal for building frameworks, but choose planed wood where a smooth finish is important. Wood should be straight and relatively knot-free. The surface should also be undamaged.

When building a framework of critical thickness (such as the basic shower partition unit on page 22) you may find it difficult to obtain wood of exactly the required thickness. If so, buy wood that is slightly oversized and plane it down.

After building, a fine surface can be obtained by sanding, either by hand with sanding paper wrapped around a sanding block, or by using an electric orbital sander. In both cases, start with medium-grade sanding paper and finish with fine,

and only sand in line with the grain, rather than across it, as this can scratch the wood.

Wood finishes If a varnish, wax polish, or paint finish is required, it can be applied easily with a brush (or rag). An alternative, often used by professional furniture makers, is to finish woodwork with a quick-drying cellulose lacquer, which can be applied with a paint sprayer. Before spraying, make sure that any holes are filled with stainable wood filler, and stain the surface, if required, before sanding it smooth. The first coat of lacquer is applied as a sealer. Leave it to dry for 30–60 minutes, then rub down the surface with fine sanding paper wrapped around a sanding block. Next, apply a second, finishing, coat of lacquer.

MEASURING AND MARKING SQUARE

Mark cutting lines lightly with a hard pencil, then use a utility knife to score against a straight-edge or try square along the rule to create a sharp, splinter-free line.

To mark lumber square, use a try square with the stock (handle) pressed against a flat side of the lumber, called the face side or face edge. Mark a line along the square, using a knife in preference to a pencil, then use the square to mark lines down the edges from the face mark. Finally square the other face side, checking that the lines join up right around the lumber.

Check a try square for accuracy by pressing it against a straight-edge. Mark along the blade, then turn the handle over to see if it aligns with the line from the other side.

If you are measuring and marking a number of pieces of the same length, then clamp them together and mark across several of them at the same time.

SPACING BATTEN

This is simply an offcut of wood, about $\frac{3}{4}$in or 1in square (19mm or 25mm square), which is used to ensure that any slats to be fixed across a frame are spaced an equal distance apart. To ascertain the length to cut the spacing batten,

simply bunch all the slats at one end of the frame. Measure to the other end of the frame and divide by the number of spaces (which you can count while you have the slats laid side by side). The resulting measure is the length to cut the spacing batten, which is used to set each slat into its exact position.

BRACING

When making a door or any similar frame, it is vital that it should be square, with corners at perfect right angles. You can ensure this by using one of two bracing methods.

3-4-5 method Measure three units along one rail, four units down the adjacent rail, then nail a bracing batten accurately to one of the unit marks. Pull into square so that the bracing batten measures five units at the other unit mark, forming the long side of a triangle. Saw off the batten ends flush with the frame but do not remove the batten until frame is fitted in place. For large doors such as those on wardrobes, fix two battens on opposing corners.

① Marking Lumber to Length and Square All Around
Mark across the face of the lumber with a utility knife held against a try square blade. Move knife around corners and mark sides, and finally mark other side to join up the lines.

② Using Spacing Battens to Space Out Slats Evenly
Bunch the slats together evenly at one end of the frame, then measure to the other end of the frame. Divide this number by the number of spaces required; cut spacing batten(s) to this length.

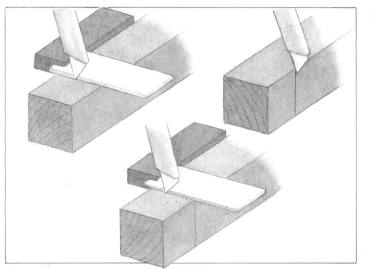

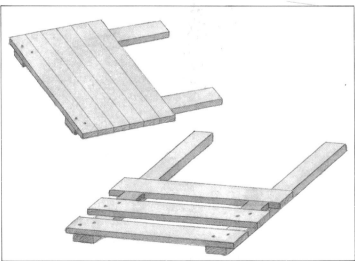

Try square method Nail a batten into one rail, pull into square by using a try square, and then nail the batten into the adjacent rail.

MAKING FOLDING WEDGES

Folding wedges are very useful for clamping large frames on a bench top during assembly. Folding wedges are always used in pairs, but more than one pair may be used to hold a large framework.

Make each pair of wedges from a piece of lumber (hardwood is ideal for this) measuring $1\frac{1}{2}$in × $1\frac{1}{2}$in × 13in (38mm × 38mm × 330mm). Make the wedges by sawing the lumber diagonally into two pieces.

To use the wedges, a wooden batten is first nailed to the bench and the item to be clamped is placed against the batten. Another batten is nailed to the bench, parallel with the first, and about $1\frac{3}{4}$in (45mm) away from the item. The wedges are now placed between the item and the second batten. The ends of the wedges are then knocked inwards with two hammers, thereby clamping the frame.

③ Bracing a Frame Square
Nail a batten across a corner of the frame so that the 3-4-5 shape triangle is formed.

SAWING AND CUTTING

Cross-cutting to length by hand Hold the lumber firmly with the cutting line (*see* **Measuring and Marking Square, page 80**) overhanging the right-hand side of the workbench (if you are right-handed). With the saw blade vertical and the teeth on the waste side of the line, draw the handle back to start the cut. To prevent the saw from jumping out of place, hold the thumb joint of your other hand against the side of the saw blade.

Rip-cutting by hand With the lumber or board supported at about knee height, start the cut as described above, then saw down the waste side of the line, exerting pressure on the down cut only. If the saw blade wanders from the line, clamp the edge of a lumber batten exactly above the cutting line on the side to be retained, and saw along it.

Using a portable power saw If the cutting line is only a short distance from a straight edge, adjust

④ Making Folding Wedges
Saw wood diagonally. Nail batten to bench; wedges fit between batten and item being clamped.

the saw's fence so that when it is run along the edge of the lumber, the blade will cut on the waste side of the cutting line. If the lumber is wide, or the edge is not straight, clamp a batten to the surface so that the saw blade will cut on the waste side of the line when it is run along the batten.

Ensuring a straight cut When cutting panels or boards using a power circular saw or a Saber saw, the best way to ensure a straight cut is to clamp a guide batten to the surface of the work, parallel with the cutting line, so that the edge of the base plate can be run along the batten. Obviously, the batten position is carefully adjusted so that the blade cuts on the waste side of the cutting line. Depending on which side of the cutting line the batten is clamped, when using a circular saw, it is possible the motor housing will damage the batten or the C-clamps holding it in place. In this case, replace the batten with a wide strip of straight-edged plywood clamped to the work far enough back for the motor to clear the clamps.

⑤ Cross-cutting to Length
Hold the lumber firmly. Steady the saw blade with your thumb joint as you start to cut.

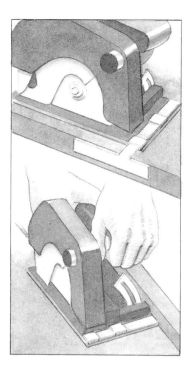

⑥ Straight Power-saw Cutting
Top **Use the rip fence of the saw if cutting near the edge.** *Above* **Cutting alongside the batten.**

⑦ Cutting with a Back Saw
Start the cut as for a hand saw. As the cut progresses keep the blade horizontal.

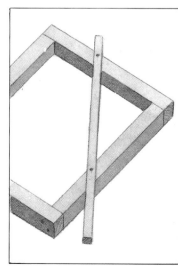

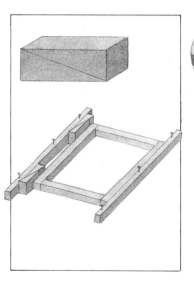

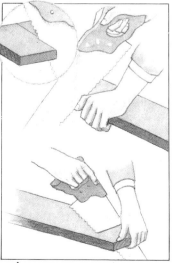

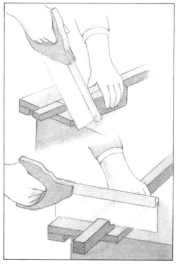

TECHNIQUES: CUTTING AND PLANING

CUTTING A CIRCLE

With a Saber saw Mark the circle on the face of the panel. If you do not have a compass, a good makeshift alternative can be made with a loop of string pivoting on a thumb tack at the circle's center. Hold a pencil vertically in the loop at the perimeter to draw the circle.

For a neat, splinter-free edge, carefully score around the cutting line with a sharp utility knife.

To start the cut, drill a hole about $\frac{3}{8}$in (10mm) in diameter just on the waste side of the line. Insert the Saber saw blade through this hole and start the cut from this point, sawing carefully just on the waste side of the cutting line. By scoring the cutting line it will be easier to follow the line and get a smooth edge.

With a coping saw Mark out the circle, score the cutting line, and drill a hole just on the waste side as above. Disconnect the blade from one end of the frame, pass the blade through the hole, and re-connect it to the frame. It will be best to clamp

the piece of work vertically when cutting the circle. The blade can be turned in the frame as necessary to help the frame clear the piece of work, but even so, with a coping saw you will be restricted in exactly how far you are able to reach away from the piece of work. If the circle is some way from the edge, use either a power Saber saw or a hand compass saw to cut it.

With a compass saw A compass saw, similar to a keyhole saw, has a stiff, triangular pointed saw blade attached to a simple handle. A very useful compass saw blade is available for fitting in a knife handle.

Because this saw has no frame, it is very useful for cutting circles and other apertures, like keyholes, anywhere in a panel.

Preparation of the circle for cutting, such as marking out, scoring, and drilling for the blade, is the same as for the other methods. When cutting with a compass saw, keep the blade vertical and make a series of rapid, short strokes without exerting too much pressure.

CUTTING CURVES

The technique is basically the same as for cutting a circle, except that there will be no need to drill a hole in order to start the cut. You can use a Saber saw, coping saw, or compass saw to make the cut. A coping saw is ideal for making this cut because most of the waste can be removed with an ordinary hand saw, since you will be cutting close to the edge of the wood, and the saw frame, therefore, will not get in the way.

CUTTING GROOVES AND SLOTS

The easiest way to cut grooves (or dados) is to use a router with a bit set to the depth required for the groove. Use a straight-sided router bit. Ideally, the router bit should be the exact width of the groove or slot, so that it can be cut from one setting. If this is not possible, then use a smaller router bit and cut the groove or slot in two or more goes. Make the first cut along the waste side of the line with a batten clamped in line with the

groove to guide the base of the router. If a deep groove is required, it may be necessary to make a shallow cut first, then a deeper one.

To cut dados by hand, start by marking out the groove with a utility knife which will ensure a neat finish. Hold the piece of work on a bench, and with a back saw, make vertical cuts just inside the marked lines to the depth of the dado. If the dado is wide, make a series of other vertical cuts in the waste wood. Now chisel out the waste, working from each side to the middle. Finally, with the flat side of the chisel downwards, pare the bottom of the dado so that it is perfectly flat.

CUTTING RABBETS

A rabbet is an L-shaped step in the edge of a piece of lumber.

To cut a rabbet by hand, use a marking gauge to mark the rabbet width across the top face of the piece of work and down both sides. Mark the depth of the rabbet across the end and sides.

Hold the lumber flat and saw down on the waste side of the marked line

---

① Straight Rip-cutting
Clamp a straight batten alongside the cutting line and saw beside the batten. A wedge holds the cut open.

② Using a Power Saber Saw
For a straight cut, clamp a batten alongside line. Cut a circle by following line.

③ Cutting Circles by Hand
1 Drill a small hole and cut circle using a compass saw. *2* Making the cut with a coping saw.

④ Chiseling a Groove
After making saw cuts at side, chisel out waste from each side. Finally pare base flat.

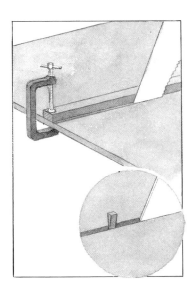

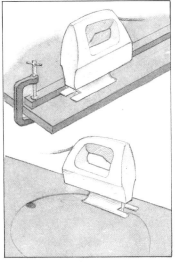

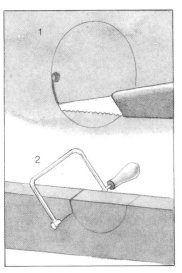

to the depth of the rabbet. Then use a chisel to cut out the waste one bit at a time along the end grain.

It is very easy to cut a rabbet using a router, and in this case it is not necessary to mark out the rabbet unless you want a guide to work to. However, do practice on scrap wood to be sure of setting the router to cut to the correct depth and width.

If using a straight cutter, adjust the guide fence on the router so that the cutter cuts to the correct width, then adjust the cutting depth so that the router will cut to the correct depth. When the router is correctly set up, simply hold it flat on the piece of work and move it against the direction of the cutter's rotation.

If you are using a cutter with a guide pin, simply adjust the depth of cut and then run the cutter along the edge of the wood to form the rabbet. The cutter will follow irregularities in the wood, so make sure the wood is perfectly straight.

MAKING A V-BLOCK

A V-block is useful for holding circular items steady while they are being worked on. Make the block from a length of 2 × 3in (50 × 75mm) S4S lumber – the actual length should be a little longer than the item to be held. The V is made to a depth of about 1in (25mm) in the 3in (75mm) side of the lumber. Cut the V using a circular saw with the blade tilted to 45°. Clamp the block firmly and fit the saw with a guide fence to keep the cut straight. Cut up one side and down the other. Practice on scrap wood while adjusting the depth and width of cut to give the correct size V-shape. Alternatively, you can use a V-cutter bit in a router. It may take two or three passes with the router to make the V to the full depth and width of the cutter.

PLANING

By hand Make sure that the plane blade is sharp and properly adjusted. Stand to one side of the work with your feet slightly apart so you are facing the work and feeling comfortable. Plane from one end of the piece of work to the other, starting the cut with firm pressure on the leading hand, transferring it to both hands, and finally to the rear hand as the cut is almost complete. Holding the plane at a slight angle to the direction of the grain can sometimes improve the cutting action.

With a power plane Remove ties and loose clothing; overalls are ideal. Wear goggles and a painter's mask. Turn the adjuster knob to set the depth to cut and start the plane. Begin with a shallow cut and increase the cutting depth if necessary. Make sure the work is clamped in place.

Stand comfortably to one side of the work and, holding the plane with two hands, set it into the work at one end and pass it over the surface to the other end. Push the plane forwards steadily; not too fast or you will get a wavy surface finish. When you have completed the work, switch off and make sure that the blades stop spinning before resting the plane down with the cutting depth set at zero.

DRILLING

To ensure that screwheads lie flush with the surface of plywood, particleboard or other material use a countersink drill bit.

To minimize the risk of splitting lumber, drill pilot and clearance holes for screws. For small screws, pilot holes can be made with an awl.

The **clearance hole** in the lumber should be fractionally smaller in diameter than the screw shank.

The **pilot hole** in the lumber to receive the screw should be about half the diameter of the clearance hole. The depth of the pilot hole should be slightly less than the length of the screw.

Drilling vertical holes To ensure vertical holes, mount the drill in a drill stand. If this is not possible, stand a try square on edge so that its stock (handle) is resting on the work alongside the drilling position, and the blade is pointing up in the air. Use this as a sighting guide and line up the drill as close as possible with the square to ensure the drill is vertical. It is also helpful if an assistant can stand back and sight along the drill and square from two sides to ensure the drill is held straight.

5 Making a V-block
Cut out a V in a block of 2 × 3in (50 × 75mm) lumber using a circular power saw tilted to cut at 45°.

6 Drilling Vertical Holes
With a drill stand, not only will the drill bit be held vertical, but depth is also controlled.

7 Freehand Drilling Guide
When drilling it can be helpful to stand a try square alongside the drill to ensure accuracy.

8 Drilling Depth Guide
There are various guides to control drilling depths, such as rings for drills, and masking tape.

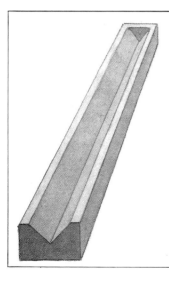

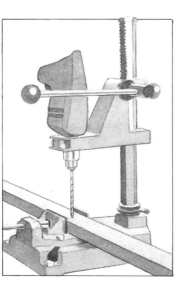

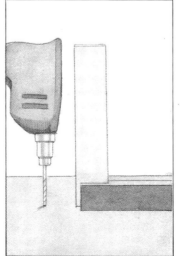

TECHNIQUES: WALL FIXTURES

SCREWING

When screwing one piece of wood to another, make sure that half of the screw penetrates into the bottom piece of wood. The screw's thickness should not exceed one-tenth of the width of the wood into which it has to be inserted. Keep screws at a distance of five times their shank diameter from the side edge of the wood, and ten times the shank diameter from its end.

NAILING

The correct length of nail to use is two-and-a-half to three times the thickness of the lumber being nailed. However, check that the nail will not pierce right through the two pieces being nailed. Wherever possible nail through the thinner piece of wood into the thicker piece.

Nails grip best if driven in at an angle ("**skew nailing**"). A row of nails should be driven in at opposing angles to each other. Framework joints are usually held by skew nailing. Clamp or nail a block of wood temporarily against one side of the vertical piece to stop it sliding as the first nail is started.

To prevent wood from splitting, particularly if nailing near an edge, blunt the points of the nails by hitting them with a hammer before driving them home. Blunt nails will cut through lumber fibers neatly, while pointed nails are more likely to push the fibers apart like a wedge, leading to splitting.

WALL FIXTURES

Solid wall The normal attachment for a solid wall is a wood screw and plastic anchor. Before drilling the fixing hole, check with a metal detector that there are no pipes or cables hidden below the surface. Drill the holes for the anchor with a masonry drill bit in an electric drill. The anchor packing will indicate the drill size to use. Switch to hammer action if the wall is hard. The screw should be long enough to go through the fixture and into the wall by about 1in (25mm) if the masonry is exposed, and by about $1\frac{3}{8}$in (35mm) into a plastered wall.

If the wall crumbles when you drill

into it, mix up a cement-based plugging compound (available from home improvement stores). Turn back the screw half a turn before the compound sets (in about five minutes). When it is hard (in about one hour) the screw can be removed and a heavy attachment made.

If your drill sinks easily into the wall once it has penetrated the plaster layer, and a light gray dust is produced from the hole, you are fixing into lightweight concrete blocks. In this case, special winged anchors for soft blocks should be used.

To make a quick, light-to-medium weight attachment in a solid wall, a masonry nail can be used. Choose a length that will penetrate the material to be attached, and pierce an exposed masonry wall by $\frac{5}{8}$in (16mm) and a plastered wall by about 1in (25mm). Wear goggles in case the hardened nail snaps when you strike it, and hammer it gently through the material to be attached and into the wall.

Lath and plaster For a strong attachment, screw directly into the

main vertical studs to which the laths are nailed. You can find these studs with a metal detector (see **Stud wall**, below).

For a lightweight attachment you can screw into the wood laths. These can be located by probing with a pointed implement such as an awl. Then insert a twin-thread wood screw. For medium-to-heavyweight attachments into lath and plaster, drill between the laths and use a cavity-wall fitting suitable for lath and plaster, such as a spring toggle, gravity toggle, or nylon toggle.

Stud wall For a strong attachment into a gypsum wallboard-covered stud wall, make a screw fixing directly into the vertical studs. You can find these by tapping the wall to check where it sounds most dense, and then probing these areas with a pointed implement until a firm background is found. Alternatively, you can make a small hole in the wall, and push a stiff wire into it horizontally until an obstruction is felt, which will be the stud. Withdraw the wire and hold it on the surface of

❶ Drilling Holes for Screws in Lumber
Drill a clearance hole in the thinner piece. Countersink this hole, then drill a hole to slightly less than screw length. *Inset* To counterbore, drill to the diameter of the screwhead to required depth, then as above.

❷ Techniques for Joining Wood by Nailing
Nail should be two-and-a-half to three times the thickness of the lumber being joined. Assemble frames on bench by nailing against batten. *Inset* Blunt nail points to avoid splitting lumber.

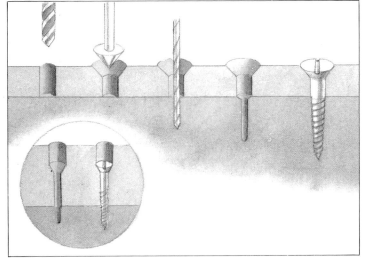

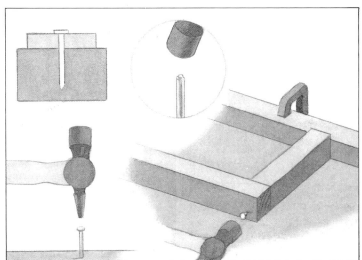

the wall so that the edge of the stud can be marked. By drilling about 1in (25mm) to the farther side of this mark, the center of the stud will be found and a screw can be inserted.

To avoid making holes in the surface of a wall, a metal detector can be used. Move it over the wall to locate a pattern of nails and mark this on the surface. Vertical rows of nails indicate a stud. Alternatively, use one of the newer electronic stud and joist detectors. This is moved over the surface to detect a change in density between the different construction materials. A change indicates the position of a stud.

If a fixture cannot be made into a stud, a lighter fixture can be made into gypsum wallboard by using a fixture designed for that material. Follow the manufacturer's instructions for the size of hole required, which can be made in gypboard with an ordinary twist drill bit.

Cavity wall Cavity walls comprise a solid inner leaf of bricks or concrete blocks surfaced with plaster and separated from the outer leaf of bricks or stone blocks by a cavity about 2in (50mm) wide.

When tapped, a cavity wall sounds solid. For fixtures, treat it is a solid wall (see page 84).

BEVELED BATTENS

These provide a very secure method of holding heavy objects on to a wall. The battens are formed by sawing a strip of wood lengthways with the saw blade set at 45°. This results in two interlocking pieces of wood. One piece, with the sloping face pointing upwards and the narrower face facing the wall, is screwed to the wall. The other piece, with the sloping face pointing downwards and the narrower side facing the item to be hung, is screwed to the item to be attached. When the item is lifted into place, the battens interlock and produce a very secure attachment.

For security, the battens should be formed by sawing a 1 × 4in (25 × 100mm) strip of lumber lengthways. Screws should be applied to the wall and into the item to be hung at about 8in (200mm) intervals. Use No 10 wood screws –

1$\frac{1}{2}$in (38mm) long into the item to be hung, and 2$\frac{1}{2}$in (65mm) long into the wall. Anchors will also be required.

ATTACHING RIGHT-ANGLED BRACKETS

These are right-angled steel strips pre-drilled for screw fixing and are useful for attaching lumber frames to walls and ceilings, as long as the brackets are positioned out of sight.

Decide where you want the bracket, hold it in place on the frame and use a pencil to mark the center of one screw fixing position. Drill a pilot hole and attach the bracket with one screw. Repeat for the other brackets. Position the frame and check that it is vertical. Mark center points of the bracket fixing holes on the wall or ceiling. Remove the frame and use a masonry drill to make anchor holes at the required positions. Press anchors into holes. Before replacing the frame and screwing brackets in place, check that brackets are still accurately positioned on the frame. Drill pilot holes for the remaining screw fixings, and insert the screws.

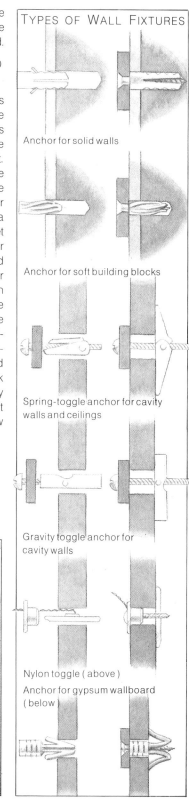

TYPES OF WALL FIXTURES

Anchor for solid walls

Anchor for soft building blocks

Spring-toggle anchor for cavity walls and ceilings

Gravity toggle anchor for cavity walls

Nylon toggle (above)

Anchor for gypsum wallboard (below)

---

③ Skew Nailing for Strength
Assemble frames by skew nailing (driving nails at an angle). The joint will not then pull apart.

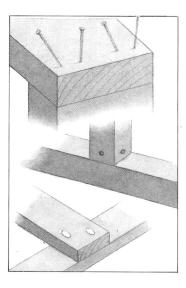

④ Using a Nailset
For a neat finish, use a nailset to drive nail heads below the surface, then fill indentation.

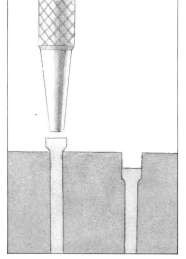

⑤ Using Beveled Battens
For a secure fixing on a wall use beveled battens made by sawing a batten lengthwise at 45°.

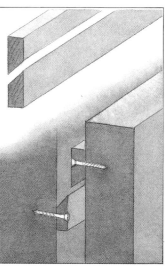

TECHNIQUES: WOOD JOINTS

WOOD JOINTS

Butt joint This is the simplest frame joint of all. The ends of the lumber to be jointed must be cut square so that they butt together neatly. Corner and "T" joints can be formed, which are glued and nailed for strength. Corrugated fasteners can also be used to hold these joints, especially where the sides of the frames will be covered to hide the fasteners. When "T" joints are being formed from inside a frame, they can be skew nailed (see page 84).

Corner joint This is a simple "knock down" fixture attached with screws; it is used to attach boards at right angles. They are described as "knock down" joints because some are in two parts for easy disassembly, and even the simple attachments can be unscrewed. They do not look very attractive, but are useful where they will be hidden – by a fascia, for example.

Miter joint Popular for making picture frames, but suitable for other

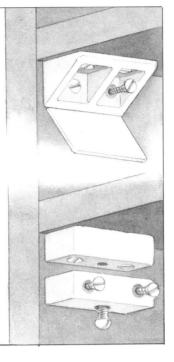

2 Corner Fitting Joints
Ideal for joining wood and boards at right angles. *Top* A one-piece fitting. *Bottom* A two-part type. Both are easily fitted using screws.

1 Simple Butt Joints
Top Corner and *below* "T" joints can be formed by skew nailing or by using corrugated fasteners.

right-angled corner joints. Cut the joint at 45° using a miter box as a guide. A simple miter joint is glued and nailed, but a stronger joint can be made using dowels, or by making oblique saw cuts into which wood veneers are glued.

Half-lap joint Also known as halving joints, these join wood of similar thickness at corners or to form "T" or "X" joints (mid-lap and cross-lap joints). Cut each piece to half its thickness. Use a try square to mark the width of the cut-outs and a marking gauge set to half the thickness of the wood to mark their depth. Be sure to cross-hatch the waste wood with a pencil so that the correct side is removed. To form an end-lap joint, saw down as for making a tenon joint (see page 88). To form a mid- or cross-lap, saw down on each side of the "T" cut-out to the depth of the central gauge line, then chisel out the waste.

Dado joint Used mainly for shelving, this is basically a slot into which a shelf fits. The "through" dado joint

3 Types of Half-lap Joints
Top A corner-lap joint. *Bottom left* A mid-lap joint. *Bottom right* A cross-lap joint.

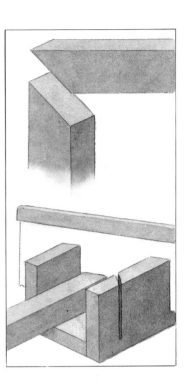

5 Cutting Miter Joints
Miters make right-angled corner joints. Using a miter box as a guide for ensuring a 45° angle, cut out the joint with a back saw.

4 Forming a Half-lap Joint in Lumber Battens
Mark width of the cut-out. Mark half the thickness of the wood with a marking gauge. Cross hatch area to be removed. Saw down sides with a back saw, then chisel out the waste.

⑥ Forming Miter Joints
Top Glue and nail together a simple miter joint. *Bottom* Reinforce the joint with a corner block, dowels, or wood veneer.

⑧ Types of Dado Joint
Top A through dado joint. *Middle* A through dado joint on the side of a central support. *Bottom* A corner dado joint.

⑦ Stages in Forming a Through Dado Joint
Mark width of the dado according to the thickness of the wood being joined. Use a utility knife. Mark depth with a marking gauge. Cut down the sides with a back saw. Chisel out the waste, working from both sides to the middle.

goes to the full width of the shelf, while a "stopped" dado joint is taken only part of the way across the board. Chisel the waste away from each side. In the case of a stopped dado, chisel the waste from the stopped end first. If you have a router, it is easier to cut a dado joint by running the router across the board against a batten clamped at right angles to the board to guide the router accurately.

A rabbet joint is similar to a dado joint at the top of a board, and can be cut in a similar way (*see* **Cutting rabbets, page 82**).

Bare-faced rabbet-and-dado joint This type of dado joint, used at the corners of a frame, is a much stronger joint than the common butt joint or lap joint because the rabbet of one piece is held in a dado cut in the other piece. The joint will be held just with good aliphatic resin wood-working glue, and by nailing or screwing down through the top into the upright. However, because of the short grain of the outside of the dado, this piece is left overlong while the joint is made, and then the "horn" (the excess timber) is cut off neatly, flush with the side of the joint. The rabbet should be no thicker than half the width of the lumber being jointed.

Carefully mark out the joint with a utility knife, a try square, and a marking gauge. The depth of the dado (groove) should be about one-third to a half the thickness of the upright. Cut the sides of the dado to the required depth using a back saw held vertical, or a carefully set circular saw. Clamping a batten alongside the dado will help to keep the cut straight. Remove the waste with a chisel, working from both sides to the middle, and holding the chisel with the flat side downwards. Alternatively, cut the dado with a router (*see* **Cutting grooves and slots, page 82**).

Mark out the vertical piece so that the rabbet will exactly fit in the dado. Use a marking gauge to mark out the rabbet. The rabbet is cut with a router or with a hand saw and chisel to form the tongue (*see* **Cutting rabbets, page 82**).

⑨ Stages in Making a Bare-faced Rabbet-and-dado Joint
Leave a "horn" of surplus lumber to support the short grain which will be on the outside of the groove. Mark width of piece being joined. Mark and cut dado as before. Saw off horn.

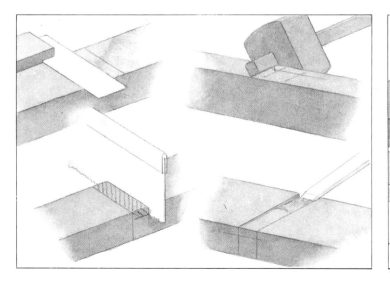

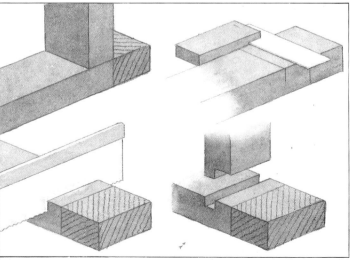

TECHNIQUES: WOOD JOINTS

Mortise and tenon joint A mortise and tenon joint can be marked out with a mortise gauge. Mark out the tenon (the tongue) so that it is one-third of the thickness of the piece of wood. The mortise (the slot) is marked at the same width in the other piece. The length of the mortise should match the width of the tenon being fitted. Drill out most of the waste with a series of holes using a drill bit slightly smaller than the mortise width. Working from the center, chop out the mortise with a chisel to the depth required. If making a through joint (in which the end of the tenon is visible), turn the wood over and complete the mortise from the other side.

Hold the tenon piece upright, but sloping away from yourself, secure in a vise, and use a back saw carefully to cut down to the shoulder. Then swivel the wood around to point the other way, and saw down to the other side of the shoulder. Next, position the wood vertically and cut down to the shoulder. Finally, place the wood flat and saw across the shoulder to remove the

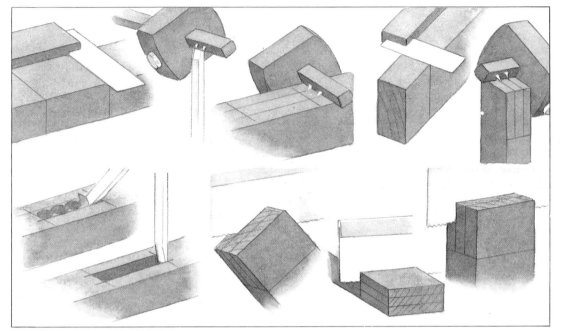

2 **Marking and Cutting a Mortise and Tenon Joint**
Mark the length of the mortise slot to match the size of the rail being joined. Set the mortise gauge to the width of the chisel being used to cut out the mortise slot. (Chisel should be about one-third the width of wood being joined.) Use the mortise gauge to mark the mortise, and also the tenon, on the rail. Drill out the mortise and complete the cut with a chisel. Use a back saw to cut out the tenon.

1 **Mortise and Tenon Joints**
Top A common or stopped mortise and tenon joint. *Below* Through mortise and tenon joint.

3 **Making a Haunched Mortise and Tenon Joint**
Leave rail over-long. Mark out as before but allow for shoulder at top. Cut mortise slot, then saw down sides of a shoulder. Finish mortise using a chisel. Cut tenon as shown.

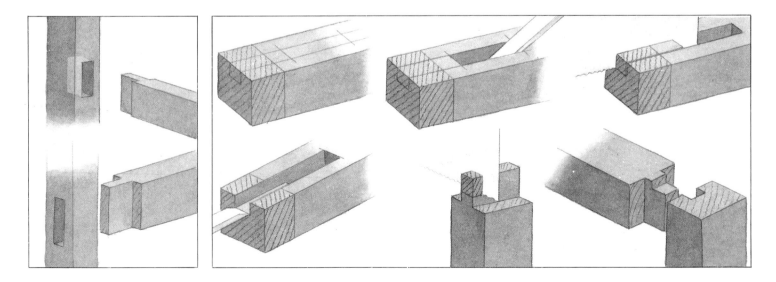

waste. Repeat for the waste on the other side of the tongue. Check that the two pieces fit well before gluing and assembling the joint. For added strength and a better appearance, cut small additional shoulders at each end of the tenon. These joints are the type used in the Wardrobe with Hinged Doors project (see page 34 for instructions).

Haunched mortise and tenon joints For joints at the corner of a large frame, such as the doors in the Japanese Wardrobe project (page 52), a square "haunch" or shoulder can be left in the tenon to increase its effective width and considerably strengthen the joint.

The joint is marked out with a try square, utility knife, and marking gauge as for an ordinary mortise and tenon, but allowance is made for a square shoulder at the top as shown in the diagram.

To prevent the small amount of cross-grain lumber above the mortise from being pushed out when the mortise slot is cut, the rail is left over-long at this stage to create a "horn"

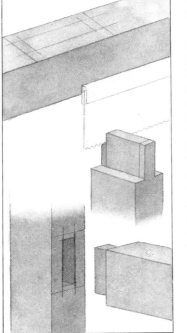

⑤ Shouldered Tenon Joint
For enhanced strength and appearance, cut small additional shoulders at each end tenon. Do this by sawing down.

④ Making a Bare-faced Mortise and Tenon Joint
Tenon is offset to one side. Mark and cut as shown here.

which is cut off after the joint has been made and assembled.

Bare-faced mortise and tenon joint If the tongue of a tenon joint is offset to one side, this produces a bare-faced tenon as shown in the diagram. This produces a strong joint where narrow rails, such as the trellis rails in the Japanese Ward-robe doors (page 52), meet the thicker frame rails. The mortise slots in the frame rails can be cut farther back from the front edge for extra strength, and the bare-faced tenons of the trellis rails allow the front faces of these rails to lie flush with the front face of the door.

A bare-faced tenon is cut in the same way as a half-lap joint (or halving joint).

Dovetail joint A dovetail joint is made so that the "pins," which are the protruding fingers, interlock in both parts of the joint, giving a joint of great pull-out strength. The joint can only come apart in the same way as it was assembled.

A sliding bevel is used to mark out

a central dovetail pin on one rail, and the dovetail shape is cut out using a dovetail saw or fine-toothed back saw to leave a central pin.

The thickness and shape of the pin is marked on the other piece, called the "post," and the marks are extended on to the ends using a try square. The post is held upright and the waste inside the two outer pins is cut out using a dovetail saw, while a coping saw is used to cut across the bottom of the waste. The sides are pared down to size with a chisel.

⑥ Marking Out and Cutting a Dovetail Joint
Mark a line the thickness of the matching piece. Using a mortise gauge, mark top of the pin. Mark sides of pin with sliding bevel set at slope of 1 in 6. Cut pin with back saw. Hold pin on other piece. Mark dovetail and cut out waste with back and coping saws. Pare base accurately with chisel to achieve good fit.

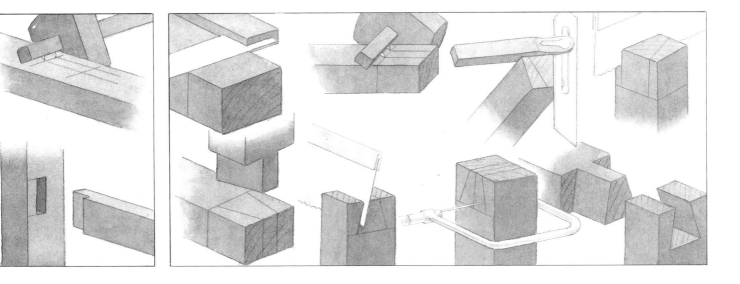

Dowel joint Dowels are a strong, simple, and hidden means of joining wood together.

Use pre-cut grooved dowels with beveled ends (*see* **Materials, page 79**). These range from $\frac{1}{4}$in (6mm) diameter by 1in (25mm) long to $\frac{3}{8}$in (10mm) by 1$\frac{1}{2}$in (38mm). The dowel length should be about one-and-a-half times the thickness of the wood being jointed. If you need to use doweling of a larger diameter (as used in the cupboard door frames in the Tiled Kitchen or for the Alcove Shelves and Cupboards), cut your own lengths of dowel. Cut grooves down the length of dowel to allow glue and air to escape, and bevel the ends. The dowel lengths should be twice the thickness of the wood being joined.

On both pieces of wood, use a marking gauge to find the center line, and mark with a pencil. Drill the dowel holes to half the dowel length with the drill held in a drill stand, or aligned with a try square stood on end. Drill the dowel holes in one of the pieces to be jointed, insert center points in the holes, then bring the two pieces of the joint together so they are carefully aligned. The center points will make marks in the second piece of wood where the dowel holes should be drilled. Drill the holes to half the length of the dowels, plus a little extra for glue. Where dowels are used for location rather than strength, such as for joining worktops, set the dowels three-quarters into one edge and a quarter into the other.

Put glue in the holes and tap the dowels into the holes in the first piece with a mallet. Apply glue to both parts of the joint; bring them together and clamp them in position until the glue has set.

GLUING

All joints are stronger if glued. Make sure that surfaces to be joined are clean and well-fitting. Clamp surfaces together while the glue is setting, but not so tightly that all the glue is squeezed from the joint. Use waterproof glue for joints that may be subject to dampness. If the parts do not fit tightly, use a two-part resorcinol glue.

1 Types of Dowel Joint
Dowels can join panels edge to edge and join frames at corners. They can be hidden or have ends exposed.

2 Dowels to Join Panels
Right Mark dowel positions. Drill holes, insert center points. Mark second piece.

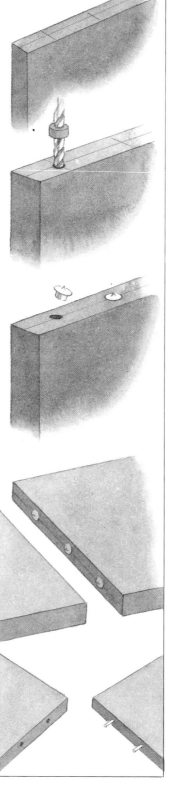

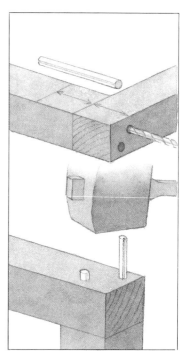

3 Making a Doweled Frame
If edge of frame will not be seen, drill holes for dowels after making frame. Hammer dowels home; cut ends flush after glue dries.

4 Using a Doweling Jig
If dowels are to be hidden, a doweling jig makes it easy to drill holes that align in both pieces.

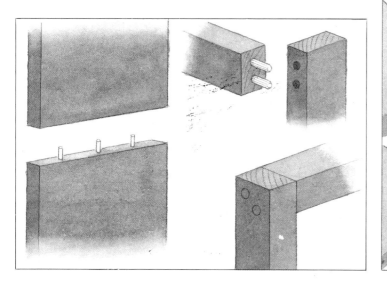

SCRIBING AND LEVELING

Scribing long lengths When you are fitting a worktop, horizontal panel, shelf, or vertical panel to a wall, you are likely to find that it will not touch the wall at every point since it is extremely unlikely that the wall will be flat and square. To avoid such gaps, it is necessary to scribe the item to the wall.

Hold the item in place and as close to its final position as possible. If it is a worktop, make sure that it is level and at right angles to whatever is next to it. If it is an upright, make sure that the front edge is held plumb. Where the gap is at its widest, pull the panel forward so that the gap is 1in (25mm). Take a block of wood 1in (25mm) long and place it on the panel, against the wall, at one end. Hold a pencil against the other end of the block, and draw the pencil and block along the wall so that the pencil makes a line, which reproduces the contours of the wall.

With a Saber saw or a compass saw, cut along the line. Where the line is too close to the edge to saw, shape the panel to the line using a tool such as a Surform or a wood rasp. Press the panel against the wall and check that it fits neatly all the way along.

Scribing in alcoves It is more difficult to scribe in an alcove because a horizontal panel will usually fit neatly only *after* it has been scribed to the walls.

Using a large wooden square (you can make one from lumber battens following the 3-4-5 principle of producing a right-angled triangle [see page 80]), find out if one, or both, of the side walls are square and flat. If they are, you can carefully measure between them at the required height of the worktop. Then saw off the ends of the worktop to this length and position it, before finally scribing it to the rear wall as described above.

If the side walls of the alcove are not square, you can mark out the worktop using a cardboard template (*see* **Using templates**) of each side wall and part of the rear wall which you then scribe to fit.

Using a contour gauge This device (*see* **Tools, page 74**) is used for reproducing a complicated shape and is useful if you have to fit, for example, a worktop around something such as a decorative wood molding. It comprises a row of movable pins or narrow plastic strips held in place by a central bar. When pressed against a shape, the pins follow the outline of the shape. The contour gauge is then held on the item to be fitted and the shape transferred to it by drawing around the contour gauge with a pencil. After use, realign the pins.

Using templates When cutting around an awkward-shaped object, such as a pipe, it is a good idea to make a template of the obstruction. Make the template from cardboard or thick paper. Cut and fold the template to make it as accurate as you can. When you are satisfied that you have a good fit, place the template on the item to be fitted, and mark around it to produce a cutting line. Alternatively, glue the template in position and cut around it.

Leveling battens When attaching battens to a wall with masonry nails, first lay the battens on the floor and drive the nails almost all the way through them. On the wall, use a carpenter's level to position the batten horizontally and draw a pencil line along the top edge of the batten. Hold the batten in position and drive a masonry nail at one of the ends part of the way into the wall. Check that the top of the batten aligns with the guide line, then rest the carpenter's level on the batten and, with the bubble central, drive a nail into the wall at the other end of the batten. Make sure that the batten is level, then drive in all the nails.

If attaching the batten with screws, drill clearance holes in the batten as above and, with a pointed tool, mark the wall through a screw hole at one end of the batten. Drill and anchor the wall at this point (*see* **Wall fixtures, page 84**) then screw the batten to the wall. Level the batten as above, mark the other screw positions, then remove the batten and drill and anchor the wall. Finally, screw the batten in place.

⑤ Scribing Long Lengths to Fit Against a Wall
Where gap is widest pull panel forwards so gap is 1in (25mm). Hold pencil against 1in (25mm) wide block; move block and pencil along wall to draw cutting line. Cut along this line.

⑥ Attaching Leveling Battens to a Wall
If attaching with masonry nails drive these into battens first. Hold batten in place and mark wall. Holding batten on marked line, insert nail at end. Recheck level; drive in other nails.

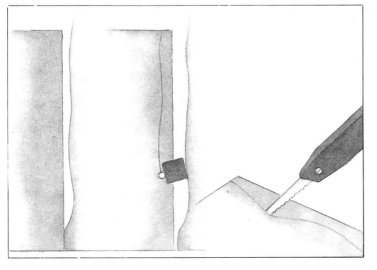

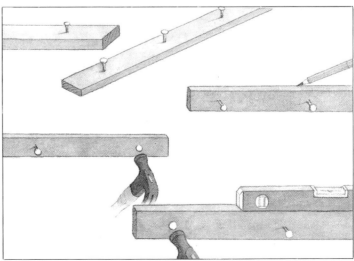

TECHNIQUES: FITTING DOORS AND HINGES

Leveling partition units Floors are rarely level, so that when installing units you must work from the highest spot in the room. Temporarily place the units in position. Take a long, straight batten and place this on top of them. Place a carpenter's level on the horizontal batten, to find the highest unit. Work from this unit and bring all the other units to this level by shimming pieces of scrap wood underneath them.

Finding verticals Use a plumb line to mark a vertical line on a wall. Tap a nail into the wall where you want the vertical to be, and tie the plumb line to it. When the line is steady, hold a scrap of wood on the wall so it just touches the string and mark the wall at this point. Repeat the procedure at a couple of other places. Alternatively, rub the plumb line with chalk. When it stops swinging, press it against the wall to leave a vertical chalk line.

HANGING DOORS

Hinged cupboard or wardrobe doors There are two ways to fit hinged doors; they can be **inset** to fit between side frames, or they can be **flush overlay** where the doors cover the side frames.

Sliding cupboard and wardrobe doors Small doors slide in double U-channel tracks made from lumber or plastic. Shallow U-channel track is fitted along the bottom front edge of the opening and a deeper track is fitted at the top, to the underside of the front edge. The grooves in the track should match the door thickness and it is important to fit the top track exactly vertically above the bottom track. Make sliding doors so that they overlap each other by about $1\frac{3}{4}$–2in (45–50mm). Their height should be the distance from the bottom to the groove in the top track, plus $\frac{1}{4}$in (6mm). After assembly of the frame unit, the door can be fitted by lifting it up and into the top track, and then slotting it into the bottom track.

Heavier doors must be hung using an overhead- or bottom-track roller system. Fitting is usually straightforward if you follow the manufacturer's instructions. Even if the track has not been fitted exactly horizontal, there is usually a means of adjusting the doors so that they move and close smoothly.

FITTING HINGES

Inset doors **Flush hinges** are the easiest to fit. They are simply screwed to the edge of the door and the frame, and require no recessing. However, they cannot be adjusted after fitting. The inner flap of the hinge is screwed to the edge of the door, while the outer flap is screwed to the inner face of the frame.

Attach the hinges at equal distances from the top and bottom of the door. With a tall or very heavy door, fit a third hinge centrally between the other two. Mark the hinge positions on the edge of the door with the hinge knuckle (joint) in line with the door front. Drill pilot holes and screw on the inner flap. Hold the door in place or rest it on something to raise it to the correct height, making sure that it is accurately aligned at the top and bottom, and mark the positions of the hinges on the frame. Remove the door and extend these lines using a try square. Hold the door against the frame so it is in an open position, and screw the outer hinge flaps in place, so that they match up with the guide lines.

Butt hinges are conventional flapped hinges and are attached in the same way as flush hinges, except that the hinge flaps are recessed into the lumber using a chisel or router. Mark out the hinge positions as for flush hinges, making sure that the hinges are not positioned so that the fixing screws will go into the end grain of cross members and be likely to pull out.

The length of the hinges are marked out first, using a utility knife, then the width of the hinge and the thickness of the flap are marked using a marking gauge. With a chisel held vertical, and a mallet, cut down around the waste side of the recess, then make a series of vertical cuts across the full width of the recess. Remove the waste by careful chiseling, then finally pare the bottom of the recess flat using the chisel held flat-side downwards.

① Fitting Sliding Door Track
Heavy doors are best hung on bottom track. Track screws to floor and rollers are inset in door bottoms.

② Fitting a Flush Hinge
Flush hinges are very easy to fit. Screw the outer flap to the frame and the inner flap to the door.

③ Fitting Face-fixed Concealed Hinges
This hinge is simply screwed to the inside face of the door and frame.

④ Fitting Recessed Concealed Hinges
Blind hole is drilled for hinge body. The base plate arm is adjustable.

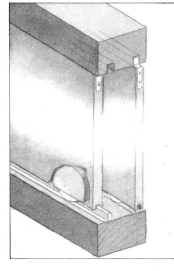

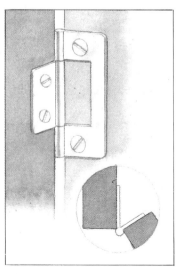

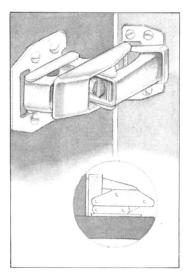

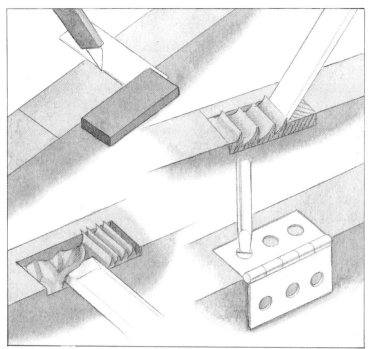

⑤ The Stages in Fitting a Butt Hinge
Using a try square and a utility knife, mark out the length of the hinge. With a marking gauge mark width and thickness of hinge flap. With chisel vertical, cut around outline of hinge. Make series of cuts across width of recess. Pare out the waste, then check that the flap lies flush. Once this is done, screw the butt hinge in place.

Flush overlay doors Modern, adjustable **concealed hinges** are the most commonly used. Some types are face-fitted and simply screw in place on the inside face of the door, but usually a special Forstner bit is used to drill a wide, flat-bottomed hole for the hinge body in the rear surface of the door. Next the base plate is screwed to the side frame. Finally, the hinge is attached to the base plate and the adjusting screws are turned until the door fits perfectly.

FITTING CATCHES

With conventional hinges, **magnetic catches** are a popular choice. The magnet is fitted to the side of the cabinet and the catch plate is then positioned on the magnet. The door is closed onto the catch and pressed hard so that the catch plate marks the door. The door is opened and the catch plate is simply screwed to the door in the correct position.

Ball catches are very neat devices. On the central edge of the door a hole is drilled to accept the body of the ball catch, which is pressed into place. The door is closed and the ball marks the edge of the cupboard. The door is opened and the striker plate carefully positioned to coincide with the center of the ball. If you are recessing the striker plate, its outline should be drawn around, using a utility knife. The strike plate is then recessed into the cabinet so that it lies flush with the surface enabling the catch to operate smoothly.

FITTING DOOR LIFT MECHANISMS

With the type we use in the Wardrobe with Hinged Doors project (page 34), the mechanism is screwed to the side face of the frame just below the top of the wardrobe, and just inside the front edge. It is held with three screws. The lift-up flap is screwed to the opening part of the mechanism with two screws, the top screw being fixed down from the top edge of the flap by the thickness of the wardrobe top plus $1\frac{1}{8}$in (28mm). This ensures that the flap opens without damaging the wardrobe front or the ceiling.

⑥ Magnetic Cupboard Catch
A magnetic catch is screwed to the inside face of a cabinet and the catch plate is screwed to the frame.

⑦ Fitting a Ball Catch
Drill door edge centrally for ball catch body which is pressed in place. Striker plate fixes to frame.

⑧ Fitting Top-hinged Door Lift Mechanism
Two types of door lift mechanism are shown below. On the left is a combined hinge and stay as used in the Wardrobe with Hinged Doors project. Also shown is a conventional stay.

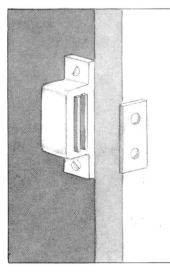

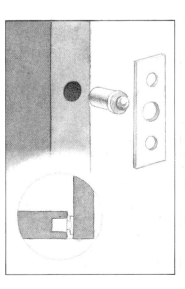

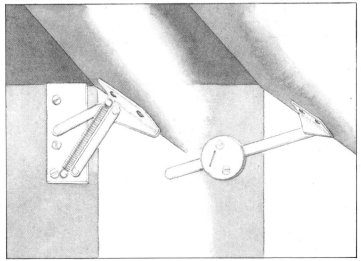

TECHNIQUES: TILING

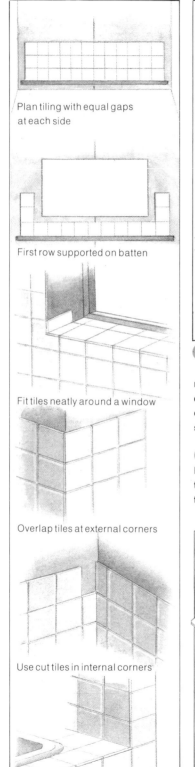

Plan tiling with equal gaps at each side

First row supported on batten

Fit tiles neatly around a window

Overlap tiles at external corners

Use cut tiles in internal corners

Planning When tiling, accurate laying out is essential. The tiles must be applied absolutely level, and, after tiling, no cut edges should show. Only factory-glazed edges, or half-round edge (bullnose) tiles which are made to be seen, should be visible. With the frames of the shower partition (page 22) note that the frame width is designed so that the front face tiles exactly cover the ends of the frames and the edges of the tiles glued to each side. Tiles on the side panels are arranged so that cut tiles are right at the back of the units. Similarly, if any tiles have to be reduced in height, these cut tiles should be at floor-level where they will be less noticeable.

When tiling a plain wall, centralize the tiles on it, using cut tiles of equal width at each end. If the wall has a prominent window, arrange the tiles to give it a neat border. In both cases, adjust the height of the tiles by having cut tiles at floor or baseboard level. Plan your tiling scheme so that part-tiled walls and low vertical surfaces, such as the side of a bathtub, have whole tiles on the top row. You may have to compromise on the best overall arrangement for the room. To deal with window reveals (recesses), have glazed edges visible around the front of the reveal, and have cut tiles butting up to the window frame.

Laying out Start by making a gauging rod. This is simply a length of straight lumber about $\frac{1}{2} \times 1\frac{1}{2}$in (12 × 38mm), on which pencil lines are drawn to indicate tile widths, including spacers. To mark the lines, lay out a row of tiles along the gauging rod, with spacers between them – unless tiles incorporating spacers are being used. Draw a line across the gauging rod to coincide with the center of each joint. If rectangular tiles are used, a second rod will be required for tile heights.

Use the gauging rod(s) to lay out accurately the tile positions. When you are satisfied with the arrangement, nail a straight lumber batten (about $\frac{1}{2} \times 1\frac{1}{2}$in [12 × 38mm]) horizontally across the full width of the area to be tiled to support the first row of complete tiles. Next, nail vertical battens at each side to support

1 Tools for Tiling
Top to bottom **Adhesive spreaders – metal and plastic; scoring tool; cutting pliers; tile nippers; heavy-duty cutter; spacers; file; saw; grout spreader.**

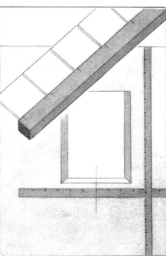

2 Making a Gauging Rod
Lay out a correctly spaced row of tiles and on a batten accurately mark tile widths including spacers.

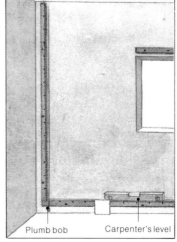

3 Setting out the Wall
Centralize tiles on a dominant feature like a window, and fix batten one tile height above floor.

Plumb bob   Carpenter's level

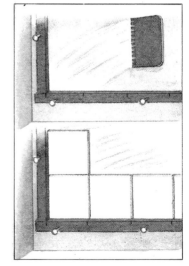

4 Starting to Attach tiles
Also fix vertical battens at each side. Spread adhesive in corner and press tiles firmly into place.

the last row of complete tiles at the sides and to keep the tiling square. Use the gauging rods to mark off on the wall battens the exact tile widths and heights, as this will help you to keep the tiling square. If you are tiling a plastered wall, nail the tiling battens with lightly driven-in masonry nails. If tiling on wood or plywood use common nails.

TILING TOOLS

Adhesive spreader A simple notched plastic tool which evenly spreads a bed of tile adhesive.

Tile cutter There are various types of tile cutters available. Some resemble a pencil and have a tungsten-carbide tip which is drawn across the tile to score the surface where the break is required. A better type is a cutter resembling a pair of pincers. This has a cutting wheel to score a cut line, as well as jaws between which the tile is placed before the cutter handles are squeezed, pincer-like, to make the cut. A heavy-duty cutter for thick, large tiles consists of a jig with a cutting-lever arm.

Tile saw Consists of a tungsten-carbide rod-saw blade fitted into a frame. It will cut tiles to any shape: L-shaped, curved, etc. The tile to be sawn is clamped in a vise.

Tile spacers Nowadays it is common for tiles to be supplied with plain edges, rather than with built-in spacer lugs molded on the edges of the tiles. Spacer tiles are simply butted together and are automatically evenly spaced as they are positioned. However, with plain edge tiles it is important to place spacers between the tiles as they are positioned. This creates even gaps for grouting between the tiles.

Tile nippers A plier-like device for removing narrow strips which are too small to be handled by a conventional cutter. It will also cut shaped tiles.

Tile-file Useful for cleaning up sharp and uneven edges of a cut tile.

Grout spreader Flexible rubber blade for spreading grout cement into joints.

Sponge For cleaning away adhesive and grout from the surface of a fixed tile.

Tiling process Establish tile positions by laying out, then begin tiling in a bottom corner and spread adhesive over about 1 square yard. Rake it out evenly using the notched spreader supplied with the adhesive. Working from a corner, press the tiles into the adhesive with a slight twisting motion. If tiles without spacers are used, hold them evenly apart with plastic wall-tile spacers. These can either be pressed well into the joints and left in place, or they can protrude from the surface, in which case they can be pulled out after an hour or so and re-used elsewhere. Fit whole tiles only: tiles cut to fit around obstacles can be fitted later.

Cutting edge tiles Wait for 12 hours after the main area of tiling has been completed, before removing the setting-out battens. Tiles can then be cut to fill the gaps around the perimeter. Measure the space into which the tile is to fit, remembering to allow for the spacers between tiles. Use a tile cutter to cut a straight line across the surface of the tile, then smooth rough edges using a tile file. Use a notched spreader to

apply adhesive direct to the back of the tile, and press it into place.

Cutting around difficult shapes To cut around a pipe, snap the tile along the center line of the pipe, then score the pipe's outline on the surface. For a neat finish, saw around the pipe outline using a tungsten-carbide rod-saw held in a conventional hacksaw frame. Alternatively, nip away the pipe cutout by snapping off small pieces of the tile, using tile nippers or a pair of pliers. Tiles to be laid around basins and window openings can also be scored along the cutting line and then nipped. Alternatively, the cutout can be sawn out, which is likely to avoid breakages if the part to be cut out is close to the edge of the tile.

Finishing off Once the tiles are firm they should be grouted with a waterproof grout applied with a rubber spreader. When the grout is just beginning to set, use a small rounded stick to press the grout into the joint lines, then wipe off the excess grout with a damp sponge. When the grouting has dried, polish the tiles' surface with a dry duster.

⑤ **Cutting Tiles to Size**
Score along glazed side, then break tile along line using a cutting tool. Saw awkward shapes.

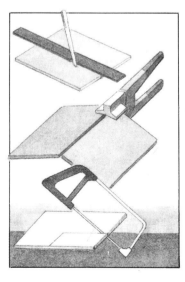

⑥ **Cutting Around Pipes**
Mark position of hole on face of tile. Snap tile along center line. Score outline, then nip out waste.

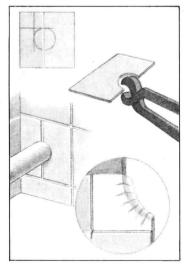

⑦ **Grouting Tiles to Finish**
Use rubber blade squeegee to press grout into joints. As grout sets, press rounded stick along joints.

⑧ **Drilling a Hole in Tiles**
Stick masking tape on drill point. Use masonry drill bit. Switch to hammer action when tile drilled through.

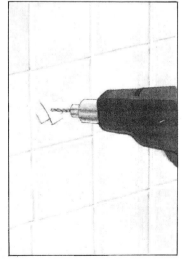

INDEX

ACKNOWLEDGMENTS

The publisher thanks the following photographers and organizations for their kind permission to reproduce the photographs in this book:

6 left Rodney Hyett/Elizabeth Whiting & Associates; **6** center Fritz von der Schulenburg; **6** right Fritz von der Schulenburg; **7** Friedhelm Thomas/Elizabeth Whiting & Associates; **8** above Tim Street-Porter/Elizabeth Whiting & Associates; **8** center Ken Kirkwood (designer David Pocknell); **8** below Vogue Living (Geoff Lung); **9** left Jean-Pierre Godeaut; **9** above right Andreas von Einsiedel/Elizabeth Whiting & Associates; **9** center right Tim Street-Porter/Elizabeth Whiting & Associates; **9** below right Rodney Hyett/Elizabeth Whiting & Associates; **10** above Lars Hallen; **10** below Michael Crocket/Elizabeth Whiting & Associates; **11** left Camera Press; **11** above right Jean-Pierre Godeaut; **11** below right Rodney Hyett/Elizabeth Whiting & Associates; **12** left Vogue Living (Georges Seper); **12** center Richard Bryant/Arcaid;

12 right Jean-Paul Bonhommet; **13** above Richard Bryant/Arcaid; **13** below left Maison Francaise (Jean-Pierre Godeaut); **13** below center Tim Street-Porter/Elizabeth Whiting & Associates; **13** below right Rodney Hyett/Elizabeth Whiting & Associates; **14** above Simon Brown/Conran Octopus; **14** center Vogue Living/Rodney Wiedland; **14** below Wulf Brackrock/designers Titterio-Dawn for Architektur & Wohnen; **15** Gabriele Basilico/Abitare.

Special Photography by Hugh Johnson and Simon Lee for Conran Octopus.

Hugh Johnson 16–19, 35, 45–9, 54–5, 61, 64–5.

Simon Lee 25, 34, 36–7, 41–3, 50–2, 62, 69, 71.